The O.C. Equation™

The
O.C.
Equation™

Unleashing Your Employees' Passion,
Potential & Performance
Through Organizational Culture

Cindy Beresh-Bryant SPHR, SHRM-SCP, RCC

Yooper Publications ®

For information contact: Yooper Publications ®, P.O. Box 158262 Nashville, TN, 37215 or visit us at

www.YooperPublications.com

Cindy Beresh-Bryant's Books may be purchased for educational, business or sales promotional use. For information please write: HR Solutions by Design 4451 Dugger Rd., Suite 101, Culleoka, TN 38451

Cover design by Roy Roper (wideyedesign.net)
Editing by Norma J. Shirk
Creative, marketing and publishing consultation by Stephanie Huffman, Epiphany Creative Services
Printed in the United States of America by www.Self-Publishing.com
Library of Congress Cataloging-in-Publication Data
    Library of Congress Control Number: 2015940274

FIRST EDITION
The O.C. Equation™ – 1st ed.
        p. cm.

    ISBN-13   978-1-941558-12-6

1. Business & Economics 2. Workplace Culture

Yooper Publications ®
P.O. Box 158262 Nashville, TN 37215
Please visit us at www.YooperPublications.com

Distributed by Thor Distribution

15 10 9 8 7 6 5 4 3 2 1

Although the author and publisher have made every effort to provide accurate, up-to-date information, they accept no responsibility for loss, injury, bad meals, or inconvenience sustained by any person using this book.

This book is dedicated to my husband, Rob, who for 30 years has followed me all over the country supporting my career. You've been a dedicated, unrelenting confidant and partner through it all.

You were also a patient sounding board when I worked for great companies, with incredible OCs that motivated, inspired and engaged employees to greatness, but also when I worked for DOGS that had OCs that sapped the very life out of their employees.

I love you, honey.
Thanks for everything.

Let your light so shine before men,
that they may see your good works
and glorify your Father in heaven.
~ Matthew 5:16

Contents

Foreword

Dr. Kimberly A. LaFevor
Dean, College of Business-Athens State University
Retired, Human Resources and Labor Relations Director -
General Motors

There is one indisputable and unequivocal expectation that we have in our world today----change. It will and does happen. The law of change suggests, like time itself, that nothing ever remains constant and stagnant. This fundamental concept is certainly relevant in effectively managing organizations today.

Managers who embrace the idea that change will occur with or without them, understand that planning must account for this phenomena both at an operational and strategic level. They can proactively plan for change or reactively adjust to environmental forces, both internally and externally to their organization. How an organization's culture is entrenched in core values, stated and integrated philosophies, and observed actions can best position the organization for the most optimal outcomes in today's dynamic environment. Thus, the role and function of organizational culture is critical to any organization's success.

Porter's Five-Force model argues that all business planning must anticipate and proactively plan for the forces that influence it. Organizations that effectively manage the forces driving change will increase their market position against competitors. Supplier power, buyer power, competitive rivalry, the threat of substitution and new entrants into the market place require planning. Planning means assessing factors that influence change and making educated decisions about what might be expected. This planning is then translated into an organizational strategy and operational goals that are nimble, flexible, and adaptable to the business climate in which an organization operates.

One might ask, what is the role of organizational culture in making business decisions? The answer is simple, though not simplistic. Organizations that are capable of self-correction, adaptation and growth are better at handling change. Organizations that resist feedback and self-monitoring are more closed and susceptible to negative outcomes and consequences. Consider the story of the VAGA, a Swedish warship that made its maiden voyage in 1628. King Gustavus Adolphus wanted a premier ship that demonstrated the expanding power of Sweden. He personally supervised the building specifications, adding more features to make the ship more imposing. The VAGA was the largest and most heavily armed warships of its time with three levels of cannon arms. It was elaborately adorned with hundreds of sculptures, and painted with brilliant colors. It was a beautiful vision when it launched. Then it immediately sank.

What happened to the VAGA? It was top heavy and no one had considered how the many design changes would affect buoyancy and maneuverability because they didn't want to disagree with the king. The organizational culture for this project team meant that they accepted the unilateral direction of the King. It was a perfect storm that lead to calamity.

The VAGA saga can be replicated in many contemporary cautionary tales. Consider famous organizations, like Smith Corona which stuck to typewriters as data processing evolved to computers; or Blockbuster which never adapted from old VHS and DVD rentals to newer technology; or Eastman Kodak which set the standards in photography only to miss out on the digital revolution. Each company found their envious market positions in their respective industries compromised because their managers failed to embrace change, build the necessary supporting culture, and effectively leverage culture to navigate through a tumultuous business climate.

Drawing from my own experiences over 20 years serving in various capacities including Labor Relations, Organizational Development, and Human Resources in a unionized, Fortune 10 company, I have found organizational culture and its relevance and applicability to labor-management relations unquestionable. Labor peace lays the path for effective working relationships, building camaraderie and team-work, whether in a union or non-union environment. Culture provides the context for effectively engaging employees to embrace shared values and beliefs within the organization, along with the emerging informal sub-cultures, which dictate whether there will be a coercive, compromising, or collaborative business climate. The first brings compliance, the second conciliation, and the latter organizational commitment.

In this book, *The OC Equation™*, Cindy Beresh-Bryant brings a unique and valuable perspective of these forces of change and how culture is at the center of creating solutions for business success. Based on almost two decades of progressive experience in managing the human resource function for both domestic and global organizations, large and small, she offers business savvy advice that provides results-oriented solutions.

I have known Cindy for about a decade. We were introduced through a mutual friend. We quickly realized we shared similar interests in business development, scholarly work, and professional engagement. Cindy and I now work together to help HR students discern employer needs and prepare these future business leaders for their transition to the workplace. It is common to find one who has extensive business experience, professional engagement, or tenure in academia. However, Cindy has successfully accomplished pinnacles of success in each of these fronts. While she has extensive hands-on business management experience in effectively managing change, she is a valued professional leader in the Society for Human Resource Management (SHRM), and dynamic educator at the collegiate level in advanced human resource practices. As a savvy business professional and scholar her advice and perspective is highly regarded and sought after.

Cindy is in the business of enabling people to facilitate organizational change in order to achieve business success. She is an effective change leader and agent of change. If you are looking for solutions to today's business problems, she can help. If you are a manager searching for solutions that can positively and proactively contribute to unparalleled competitiveness, she provides invaluable insight in this book that provides a roadmap for positive transformation of any organization. Her critical thought and insight provides convincing evidence that in today's business climate change is inevitable and building the desired organizational culture is the key to organizational sustainability.

Part 1
You Are HERE!

Chapter 1

Clashing Cultures
Spell Disaster

"Culture is not the most important thing
– it's the ONLY thing"
~Jim Sinegal, Co-Founder and
former President & CEO, Costco, Inc.

In 2005, I spent 3 weeks in Pune, India on business. It was both a thrilling and intimidating experience. Although I stayed at an exquisite five star hotel that catered to American business people and made substantial attempts to make us feel at home, it was still evident that we were in a foreign land. One sunny, Saturday afternoon when I was completely bored looking at the four walls of my hotel room, I decided to take a walk to the local market. As I looked around, I realized that everything, and I mean EVERYTHING, about India was different - the scenery, the smells, the food, the people, the way they dress - EVERYTHING.

As you can imagine I stood out like a sore thumb walking down the street looking very American, acting very American, and expecting very American responses. After all, I didn't speak Hindi, I had blond hair, I didn't wear a sari, I didn't know their customs, beliefs or traditions and everything about me was completely different from the local Indian people. Although I had attempted to learn as much as possible about their culture before arriving, there was no doubt - I didn't fit in, I didn't belong.

In India I quickly decided there are very few, if any, rules of the road. When driving, although they had similar traffic signs and red lights, it became painfully observed there were no dividing lines separating traffic lanes and few roads were paved. When traffic lights changed from red to green, it was literally every man (and woman) for themselves. It was not unusual for a driver to drive momentarily down the wrong side of the road to maneuver around traffic or to avoid obstacles, only moving back to the "right" side of the road when oncoming traffic threatened a head on collision.

Because the driving customs were so vastly different from home, I had an Indian driver pick me up at the hotel and drive me back and forth to work during the week. My driver was constantly dodging pedestrians, cows, goats, other cars, scooters, and anything else that might wander into the road. It didn't take me long to realize that I was much better off, and far less stressed, if I just looked out the side window of the car admiring the scenery. But even that was different. I saw houses that were little more than shanty towns with no running water or electricity, I saw adults and children alike coming to the edge of the road, mere feet from traffic, to urinate or defecate in the street. I saw slaughtered, skinned animals hanging up to dry or be sold in the market with no refrigeration to ensure freshness and I saw women washing vegetables in the storm water runoff on the side of the street. There was no doubt; India had a very different culture from America.

Their "Culture", the way they do things, was completely different from our culture here in America. They have their own languages, their own goals and objectives, their own personal values and philosophies, and their own ways of doing things. Most of which were completely different from what I was accustomed to.

Webster's dictionary defines "Culture" as "*The beliefs, customs, arts, etc., of a particular society, group, place, or time*". And just as a country has their own culture, so do organizations. As a matter of fact, Webster's acknowledges organizational cultures (OC) and defines it as "*A way of thinking, behaving, or working that exists in a place or organization (such as a business)*". And, just as I felt like a fish out of water in India, when you're dropped into an unfamiliar organizational culture (OC), one that gets things done in a completely foreign way from how you would "normally" do things, you will likely feel equally out of place and awkward. For some people that feeling of awkwardness passes quickly as they assimilate and integrate into their new surroundings and adapt to their new organization's way of doing things. But others may never assimilate into the OC, especially if the organization's way of doing things goes against their personal values and philosophies, their hardwiring so to speak. They may never quite fit in, always struggling to find traction, build relationships and get results.

Take for example my own personal experience with a client a while back. I knew as the words were coming out of my mouth, there was going to be fall out, but to be honest, at the time, I simply didn't care. Then, a couple of weeks later the person who had contracted me for the job called and told me, "They don't want you back." I was devastated. But at that moment, it became clear, I wasn't a culture fit for their organization and no amount of trying was going to change that. In other words the way they did things was contrary to the way I did things and neither of us were willing to sacrifice our values or beliefs or our philosophies to make the necessary changes to assimilate together to make it work. After two years working with this client, it was obvious, although no one would admit it, that my personal and professional values and their OC clashed. We simply didn't "fit", we had different leadership philosophies, different people philosophies and different engagement philosophies and neither of us was willing to change our beliefs, values or customs to maintain the relationship and make it work.

Whether dealing with a local culture in another country or with a culture in an organization, it's imperative that there be an understanding and respect for the values and philosophies that have established it. Or to put it another way, "when in Rome, do as the Romans" because it's unlikely you're going to change the culture.

We see this kind of reaction in our daily lives and in our workplaces.

Sometimes you go into an organization with stars in your eyes, excited about new possibilities, but quickly learn the organization has a different value system and culture that doesn't support your personal needs, philosophies and values and you're not a fit. You feel like a fish out of water, struggling to perform, get along and build an effective network. Struggling to figure out how to be effective and get things done, wondering what's wrong with you. On the other hand, when you work or volunteer in an OC that suits your personal values and style, it's like lightening in a bottle – everything just fits, seemingly without effort and it feels like coming home.

But how do you know what the organization's culture is? Can you know before you decide to go to work with them? Can the OC change with management changes? How can you determine if the current OC is effective? If not, how can the OC be changed to provide a competitive advantage?

Fitting into an OC can be faked for a period of time, but eventually faking it will take its toll and in the end, it always comes crashing down – either in the crashing and burning of relationships and interactions, performance, or in someone's personal health and happiness. When the culture doesn't fit who you are, what you value and hold dear, it's an absolutely miserable experience.

We will explore all of these issues throughout this book. It is designed as a practical guide to help anyone, at any level, in any type or size organization understand the power of OC and how it can be used to unleash your employee's passion, potential and performance to create a sustainable competitive advantage in the marketplace.

What is Organizational Culture (OC)?

As previously noted, an organizational culture (OC) is like a country's culture. It's the shared traditions, beliefs, values, philosophies, and actions of the people who make up the organization. In other words, quite simply, it's **how things get done**, the way employees think and act, what forms the basis of their decisions at work.

Using a simple, but powerful equation – **The OC Equation™** - you can discover what makes up your current OC and if it aligns with and supports what your organization says it values. Once you know what your OC is, you can begin evaluating if it's effective. Does it engage employees and empower them to get results and go the extra mile? If not, the second half of the book will provide a roadmap for putting together a workable action plan to unleash your employees' passion, potential and performance and create the one true competitive advantage.

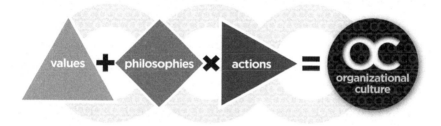

Values + Philosophies x Actions = OC]

By using **The OC Equation™** you will begin to discover what you or your organization truly values. You will be able to articulate those values through specific, detailed philosophy statements and then compare those to your actions to determine if they're consistent. Consistency is the key: for employees to emotionally and physically invest in your organization, they have to know where you stand and what you value. If you're all over the place they won't fully commit themselves, remaining on the fringes of the OC and, like a reed in the wind, waiting on cues to decide how they should behave.

For example, we've all been to Effective Communication seminars where we learned, sometimes through harsh examples, that when faced with words or actions (body language, gestures, tone, etc.) people will believe your actions every time over the words they hear. Your OC works much the same way. You can tout "values and philosophies" all you want, you can tell employees what a great place to work they have. But in the end, they will decide if they agree with your assertions based on your actions – what you actually did vs. what you said. If your words and actions are different, employees will always look to the actions to tell them everything they need to know about what you truly value.

What is Culture "Fit"?

Recently, a client whose OC is defined by getting things done based on relationships and face-to-face, personal interactions, hired a very tech savvy employee accustomed to communicating and getting things done through the use of technology – email, instant messaging, and texting. Bam! An almost instant OC clash! Their new employee was communicating in a manner that didn't "fit" the OC, creating strife and dissatisfaction among co-workers. A strife that he was completely oblivious to.

As the tech savvy employee illustrates, it's possible to have exceptional talent with the right education, experience, knowledge, skills, and abilities (KSAs) to do the job, but lose the impact and effectiveness of that talent if they aren't a culture "fit". If a highly talented employee is trying to get things done in a manner contradictory to the organization's OC (their values, philosophies, beliefs and traditions), their effectiveness will be greatly diminished simply because *how* they approach the job, their co-workers, leaders, customers and vendors doesn't fit with expectations and norms, creating high anxiety and frustration for everyone involved. While the frustration and anxiety will be recognized almost immediately, the reason seldom is because it's not something you can easily put your finger on.

With few exceptions, no one sits you down on your first day of employment (or during the interview process) and tells you about their OC. It isn't something that you can see or read even in marketing materials or the employee handbook; often emerging as an unsettling prickle,

prickle, prickle deep in your gut that something isn't quite right. Ignore OC at your peril because it has the power to propel or derail not only your career but the organization's success.

Culture fit, based on **The OC Equation™**, is when your personal values, philosophies and actions coincide with the organization's values, philosophies and actions. In other words, it is matching how things get done in an organization with how you would expect to get things done yourself. Now don't become too concerned if you experience that tell-tale prickle, it doesn't mean the organization is evil or bad or wrong and it doesn't mean you're evil or bad or wrong, it simply means there's not a proper "fit". This is why hugely successful leaders and employees at one organization can go to another organization and completely bomb out.

"Behind every successful leader is a vibrant culture that engages and energizes employees. In almost every case, that culture has been defined, shaped and personified by the leader." ~Anonymous

The Elusiveness of OC

OC is like the wind and in the case of an OC misfit that wind turns into a hurricane leaving a path of organizational and personal destruction in its wake and depending on the survivors to pick up the pieces and start again. The problem is that it's usually the best employees that jump ship. You can't shake off bad employees with a stick!

If OC can be such a competitive advantage, then why do so few leaders embrace it? OC is a difficult concept for many people to comprehend, especially those who are data driven because it's elusive and can't be directly measured like the number of widgets produced. OC, however, can be measured by the indirect outcomes of its presence – attendance, customer satisfaction, employee engagement, productivity, quality, safety, complaints, conflict, etc.

Leaders, and all employees for that matter, know they have an OC, but few have the foresight or vision to harness it and leverage it as a bona fide business tool. Most ignore it because they can't readily see it and don't believe they can make a hard measure out of it. They don't intuitively understand how or why their OC was created or how it's sustained. They aren't sure if it can or even should be changed. They feel it's too complicated and ambiguous to harness. They don't even know if it should be harnessed, and if it should, how. Worse yet, they don't know what to do with OC once it is harnessed. Shouldn't it just be ignored, they wonder, as they move on to other priorities?

Because leaders are accustomed to dealing with cold, hard facts and data, they seldom take the time or invest the energy to deal with abstractions. OC is definitely an abstraction. As a matter of fact, it's like the wind - you can't see it, grasp it, or even hold on to it, but you definitely know it's there. You can feel it and you can experience its effect on the people and environment around you. You can also harness its power to create a competitive advantage for your organization. Harnessing your OC, however, takes vision, discipline, hard work and an unwavering, intentional spirit.

High employee engagement ultimately has the power to propel an organization to outperform their competition. According to research by Towers Watson, organizations with high engagement experience have, on average, three times higher operating margin than organizations with low engagement. But unlocking the secret to engagement isn't easy – or inexpensive. One major factor in employee engagement is employees' perceived connection to the organization resulting in their willingness to use discretionary effort (go above and beyond what's expected) to get results. But how do you raise engagement? Most organization's focus is on the hard measures such as: pay, benefits, and training. But the fact is that no matter how much you pay someone, if they don't feel an emotional connection to the organization, you won't be able to unleash their passion, potential or performance.

Creating that emotional connection is about connecting employees to your OC. The shared values, philosophies, beliefs and traditions of your organization and how those translate into the decisions and actions people see every day. Because OC is so elusive, most leaders fail to harness its power. To do so requires vision, commitment and intentionality. Few leaders recognize its power or take the time and effort to think beyond the obvious to harness it and use it to their advantage. As we noted previously, every organization has an OC, but do you use it to your advantage or is it being used against you?

Harnessing the power of your OC to attract, engage and retain top talent will ultimately position your organization to outperform the competition, survive a recession, enhance your value proposition or any number of other competition crushing achievements. Forward-thinking leaders have the insight and vision to recognize that OC is just as important to success as innovative products and services, cutting-edge R&D, superior customer services, lean manufacturing, and uncompromising systems and processes.

Throughout this book we will help you eliminate the elusiveness of OC. We will teach you how to harness your organization's OC and create a competitive advantage that can't be duplicated by your competition. We will show you how to apply **The OC Equation™** to every department and decision within your organization and unprecedented results.

Not a Quick Fix

Although we will teach you the components needed to harness your OC, make no mistake; it is not a quick fix for all that ails your organization. It's not like a fancy new software program that you can buy and install one time and then walk away. Using OC as a competitive advantage takes considerable commitment, intention and discipline. Leaders must be constantly vigilant to ensure the desired OC is not only identified, but the actions of employees at all levels are consistent with the desired OC and reinforce it, protect it, and nurture it without compromise. Commitment and discipline are required especially when OC begins to slip, when it begins to once again become elusive, when things get off course, as with any other business metric, action plans must be put in place to get back to the espoused values and philosophies to ensure consistency, which in turn ensures commitment.

It takes hard work because employees at all levels have to think, speak, act and lead in such a way as to instill and reinforce the espoused values and philosophies of your OC into every other leader, manager, team member and employee so their actions demonstrate the values and philosophies and mirror your ideal and intended OC. This ensures your decisions will not only take into account the business needs and demands, but that it also takes into account employee needs and demands as they relate to the desired OC. Thus every action must be considered and calculated in terms of its impact on the OC while constantly evaluating if those actions are helping or hindering your achievement of the desired OC. Leaders who aren't willing to put in this extra effort will find themselves at the mercy of an accidental, unintentional, yet equally powerful OC driven by the most influential or manipulative employees in the organization, which will quickly reduce your desired OC to just another grandiose idea or flavor of the month.

It takes an unwavering, intentional spirit because there are times when sticking to your values and philosophies will force you to make decisions and implement actions that, in the short term, appear to defy logic and "good business sense". However, for those with the fortitude to stick with it, the payoffs are nothing short of extraordinary.

Getting it Right

During the recent "Great Recession" I flew every week to New Jersey for my job. As the recession deepened I began to notice a drop in employee morale and customer service at my airline of choice. Employees on and off the flight began behaving as though their customers were an annoyance, in some cases becoming borderline hostile and even abusive. After suffering through the effects of dwindling customer service coupled with almost weekly fare hikes I finally decided that the pain of dealing with their employees' attitudes wasn't worth it. Although my previous airline provided a direct flight into Newark, NJ, I longed to be engaged and connected to my weekly airline provider.

So I began looking for alternatives. That's when I discovered the "fun" of Southwest Airlines. I hadn't previously considered Southwest because they didn't provide service into Newark. To change airlines would mean I would have to fly into Philadelphia, Pennsylvania and then take a train to Iselin, NJ and then walk 2 blocks to the office – suitcase in tow. But with service dwindling and price increasing, the airline had finally hit the law of diminishing returns; they were no longer worth it. The idea of feeling connected and valued was more important to me than the pain and effort of multiple train rides and a short walk to the office, even in the snow!

But how did Southwest earn my business even though it cost more time and effort? It was their OC. Their OC was infectious to both employees and customers alike. Southwest has an OC with consistent values, philosophies and actions and they hire employees who share and embrace their OC. Employees demonstrated true customer service through their commitment to providing a pleasant experience no matter what the circumstances and engaging passengers in that experience.

Organizations that get it right don't worry that an employee will leave to go to another employer for a few more bucks per hour. They don't worry that they might lose customers because of a cheaper price or easier interface, because OC creates commitment, loyalty and dedication – a connection that all humans ultimately seek.

Even with years of experience working and leading great OCs and personally experiencing the power of those OCs to engage employees, inspire commitment, dedication and loyalty and get extraordinary results, I've also witnessed both personal and professional destruction when OCs go awry.

The reason you should push through the elusiveness of the OC is because it's what *really* matters – after all, it's the ONLY thing your competition can't duplicate. Turnover is expensive both monetarily and emotionally; and as previously noted, personal and organizational performance can only be maximized when the "fit" is correct. This book is about helping you learn from both my triumphs and failures so you can leverage a winning OC to outperform in your niche.

In the following chapters we will walk you through how to assess your organization's OC based on **The OC Equation™**. You'll learn how to identify your actual versus stated OC, you'll develop philosophies to back up those values and you learn how to ensure congruence and continuity and leverage your OC to crush your competition.

Hold on! You're in for the ride of your life – one that can change your future and the future of those around you – for the positive.

Chapter 2

Do You Speak "Harvard"?

Developing an OC as a Competitive Advantage Doesn't Take a Rocket Scientist

"Complexity is your enemy. Any fool can make something complicated. It is hard to keep things simple."
~Sir Richard Branson

You get up early and turn on the morning news program while you prepare for work. Some "expert" is expounding on the crisis of the moment. At first, you think you haven't had enough coffee because the expert makes absolutely no sense. Then you realize the expert has "Harvard Syndrome", a desire to impress by using twenty-five cent words and industry-speak (buzzwords) to obscure complicated concepts rather than to enlighten the audience. You turn off the TV to head out to fight rush hour traffic and you're already annoyed.

You're annoyed because the so-called "expert" on the news treated you with contempt by confusing the issues rather than helping you understand them. Why couldn't the expert explain the crisis simply and clearly? When you're attempting to diagnose, implement or change your OC it's no different – simple is better. Keep it simple or you'll lose your people and your momentum. Think about your own organization. How many great ideas, projects and programs die each year just because they are so overburdened no one can keep up with them? Your employees can't possibly embody the OC you're striving to create (and

29

they won't even try) if it's too complicated or cumbersome which means ultimately you will lose any potential competitive advantage you had hoped to gain from it. So, keep it simple.

As with most things, if it's simple, people will use it. Take for example all the weight loss plans advertised every year to an overweight American public. These plans make losing weight simple and people BUY simple: order our prepackaged meals, eat 5 times a day, plus 2 snacks and you too can obtain your ideal weight! Or consider the simplicity of Apple's devices. The sleek design of the original iPod – no complicated buttons and total integration of the computer, the software and the iTunes Store to access all the media you could ever want or need.

Steve Jobs got this concept of simplicity and built his company on that guiding principle. Under his leadership, Apple, Inc. became the epitome of simplicity—not just a superficial simplicity that comes from an uncluttered look and feel at the surface of their products. It's a deep simplicity that comes from knowing the essence (the purpose) of every product, the complexities of its engineering and the function of every component. "It takes a lot of hard work," Jobs said, "to make something simple, to truly understand the underlying challenges and come up with elegant solutions." In a 1977 marketing brochure Apple claimed, "Simplicity is the ultimate sophistication." No doubt that Jobs got it, lived and breathed it and demanded that everyone working with him also lived and breathed it – it was part of Apple's OC.

KISS – Keep it Simple, Stupid!

Throughout my career I've worked for some of the most beloved and recognized brands in the world, I have seen the power of both the Six Sigma and Lean methodologies. The Six Sigma methodology seeks to reduce variation. The reduction of variation is important because variation generates waste which in turn increases our energy and resource use to chase down and manage processes and results that are not what we want or expect. When Six Sigma is used, processes are simplified. And simple things are easier to predict, repeat and control.

Lean manufacturing also strives for simplicity. Lean principles drive a simplification of process and, often, management structure. Lean seeks to eliminate unnecessary work and waste by eliminating unnecessary steps, reducing movement and exchanges, minimizing material, and dictating a highly focused management structure for each market or product line. In other words, it simplifies the processes, equipment and decision-making.

The point is, whether your business has adopted a popular business improvement or process improvement methodology, or whether you prefer to follow your own methods, you can generate a great deal of business, process, and product improvement by following the "Simplicity Principle" – Keep it Simple, Stupid (KISS).

OC is Simple, but Not Simplistic

The Ultimate in Simplicity – Einstein's Theory of Relativity

"If you can't explain it simply, you don't understand it well enough"
~ Albert Einstein

$$E=mc^2$$

Einstein's theory of relativity, on one level, is devastatingly simple. It says that the energy (E) in a system (an atom, a person, the solar system) is equal to its total mass (m) multiplied by the square of the speed of light (c, equal to 186,000 miles per second). But on another level, like all good equations, its simplicity is a rabbit-hole into something so profound it boggles the mind.

Before Einstein, scientists defined energy as the stuff that allows objects and fields to interact or move in some way – kinetic energy is associated with movement, thermal energy involves heating and electromagnetic fields contain energy that is transmitted as waves. All these types of energy can be transformed from one to another, but nothing can ever be created or destroyed. The fact is that Einstein's simple equation brought a new understanding to the world of physics and paved the way to the creation of the atom bomb.

Figuring out your Organizational Culture (OC) isn't hard. In fact, it's incredibly simple if you can stomach the truth. **The OC Equation™**, like the theory of relativity, provides a clear map that you can actually understand and use to not only diagnose your organizational culture (OC) but figure out practical, effective changes to improve it and get results. But beware; beneath The OC Equation's™ simplicity lies a rabbit hole into values, philosophies, systems and processes, policies and procedures and internal and external actions. Its significance doesn't pave the way for the creation of a physical bomb but it does pave the way for an organizational bomb that can, by its sheer strength and power, infiltrate every cranny of your organization.

When the components of **The OC Equation™** are consistently applied and leveraged as a key business strategy, they can change the face and dynamics of your organization which allows you to attract and retain top talent and inspire performance. Employees will be perpetually engaged, deliver high performance and make decisions as if they owned the company. Organizational Culture can create a sustainable, truly proprietary competitive advantage for your organization that competitors can't duplicate.

The beauty of **The OC Equation™** is that it is simple to understand and use even as it delivers results that are not simple. Our desire for more features and more options tends to drive complexity in business, processes, products, policies, procedures and practices. But the solutions that perform the best are the ones that are simplest to understand, operate and manage. Working with employees is no different.

For example, while developing **The OC Equation™** I researched several well-known authors and institutes famous for their "intellectual horsepower" and strategic research on OC. The problem was that I couldn't understand what they were talking about although I had lived and breathed OC for more than 20 years in actual workplaces and seen firsthand the incredible impact a positive OC can have on bottom line metrics! As I reviewed their work, I found it so fraught with the "Harvard Syndrome" and so "intellectual" and complicated that no one could actually understand it, let alone implement it and know what changes to make to affect OC to drive superior business results in a "real" organization.

Their discussions of culture depended on complex equations and foreign terminology that would require business leaders to learn and implement a whole new language. The result of such an approach is a deer in the headlights look and head scratching rather than serious strategic consideration. But it doesn't have to be that way – developing and implementing a positive OC doesn't have to be complicated. But it does take a commitment to OC as part of the overall strategic plan, clarity on your organization values, disciplined intent and simple but consistent and powerful actions that actually infuse OC into the DNA of your organization to make a positive difference in engagement and performance of your people, their department and the organization.

So, like any good researcher, I didn't rely solely on my own experience. I assembled a group of trusted colleagues who personally worked in and were responsible for creating and reinforcing some of the best organizational cultures in the world to help identify and clearly articulate what it takes to create a positive OC that drives business results and what it takes to sustain that OC through business changes and leadership turnover.

Simplicity and The OC Equation™

Before we jump into how to actually "use" **The OC Equation™** in future chapters, let's explore the power of simplicity and why keeping it simple is the best approach to sustainability.

Fortunately for all of us, even if we don't speak Harvard (and I don't), creating a positive, empowering OC that supports our business strategy, goals and objectives doesn't require us to. Simply put, the components of culture (good or bad, intentional or accidental) are best represented by **The OC Equation™**:

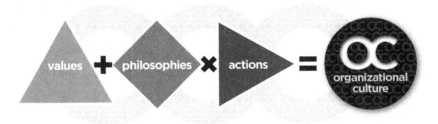

The power of **The OC Equation™** is that it is simple. But don't be lulled into believing that makes it less potent, profound, or effective. In fact, it is the simple nature of **The OC Equation™** where you find its power and the ability to leverage its components in harmony to maximize your one true competitive advantage – your people. It's an advantage your competition can't duplicate.

Your OC Is Your Competitive Advantage

If you're still on the fence as to whether organizational culture is important, consider the following facts:

- **Only 30% of American employees are engaged** – According to Gallup's State of the American Workplace: 2013 report, only 30% of American workers and 13% of global employees are engaged, or involved in, enthusiastic about, and committed to their workplace.

- **It's better to be fair than right** – Neuroscientists discovered that when employees feel mistreated, those emotions run deep and are not easily forgotten. So, if your OC emphasizes treating employees with respect and dignity it will likely reinforce one or more of the six employee needs and build loyalty and engagement. (The six employee needs are discussed in later chapters.)

- **Social interaction drives results** – Whether an introvert or an extrovert, our brains are predominately social organs and need social interaction and goals to perform at its peak. However, most OCs focus on optimizing results over people (social interactions) resulting in employees (even top performers), feeling devalued, insecure or even unfairly treated which may lead to disengagement.

Using your OC to your advantage isn't just about making employees happy or making everyone feel good. It's about getting results as discussed in more detail in Chapter 4. For now, suffice it to say, the bottom line is this: creating an empowering OC that drives employee engagement and satisfaction isn't rocket science. It's incredibly simple, but not simplistic. It takes discipline, constant vigilance and sometimes short-term financial sacrifices.

Case in point: In 2004, top leaders in a multinational organization presented their local leadership with a plan to save the plant millions of dollars over a 5 year period, which was incredibly attractive. The plan would outsource maintenance and facilities to a provider guaranteeing improved response time, improved machine uptime and improved Maintenance, Repair and Operations (MRO) cost savings. In addition, the organization negotiated with the provider to hire the current maintenance team so there would be no learning curve and no one would be out of work – they would leave one organization on Friday and report to work on Monday as an employee of the new provider.

When this plan was presented to Human Resources (HR), they hit a snag. No, it wasn't because of HR; it was because of their commitment to their culture. HR reminded the leaders that they would have to abide by the severance policy and offer every maintenance employee severance adding hundreds of thousands of dollars to the cost. Incredulous that their cost savings would be virtually wiped out in the near term, the leaders took their argument to the CEO, sure he would support the business decision. When they approached the CEO, he listened intently to their proposal and reviewed in detail their cost saving projections, impressed with the potential financial impact. When presented with the dilemma, the CEO asked one question, "On Monday morning will the affected employees work for our company or wear someone else's' logo?" The answer was clear; they would work for someone else. In less than a nanosecond, the CEO stated, "if you move forward with this plan, these employees are entitled to severance. It's not whether they have a new job on Monday or not, it's the fact that they will no longer be employed by us."

Feeling defeated, the team left his office, but the culture remained intact and employee loyalty and engagement was never stronger because the employees knew the organization not only posted values on the wall – they lived them!

The key in this particular situation was the fact that the CEO boiled the entire matter down to the bare essence in order to effectively deal with it. Developing a competitive OC happens only when you boil down your values, philosophies and actions to their essence and then develop the systems and principles to keep it simple.

So, the message here is KISS. Don't worry about speaking "Harvard" or over complicating your journey to an effective OC. You don't have to speak "Harvard" to create and maintain a positive culture that engages employees, but it has to be intentional.

The OC Equation™ in Action

1   KISS – Keep it Simple, Stupid
    – don't over complicate your OC.

2   Only 30% of employees are engaged:
    OC drives engagement > Drives results> competitive advantage.

3   Employees value being fair over being right
    – develop an OC that fuels "doing the right thing".

4   Getting to simple is HARD work,
    but simple doesn't mean simplistic!

5   If you build it (an intentional OC), they
    (results and competitive advantage) will come!

Chapter 3

The OC Equation™ – Your Formula for Creating a Sustainable Competitive Advantage

Case in Point: The Real Cost of a Real Life Culture Mis-Fit

"Your beliefs become your thoughts. Your thoughts
become your words. Your words become your actions.
Your actions become your habits. Your habits become your
values. Your values become your destiny."
~ Mahatma Gandhi

You've likely been there, you walk into an organization and you "feel" the tension. You can't put your finger on it exactly, but something's just not quite right. Many times people say all the right things, everything sounds wonderful and fulfilling, but there's a nagging feeling in the pit of your stomach that tells you all is not as it seems.

That's the way it was when I first moved to Nashville, Tennessee. I was recruited by a multi-billion dollar, privately owned corporation to come to Nashville to head up the Human Resources function for one of their divisions. The company had a long history of incredible growth and profitability and they were expanding a smaller division as part of their growth strategy into new emerging markets. Their strategy was to take a very successful mid-market product and add both low and high end product lines to their portfolio that would round out their presence in the desired market segments.

Up until this point I had had a skyrocketing career. I had been with an incredible company for almost 10 years enjoying promotion after promotion and taking on more and more responsibility. Life was good. And then along came this opportunity to be the HR lead for a $3 billion division and get back to the South in the process – what could possibly go wrong? I really had no intention of leaving my present employer when this opportunity presented itself, but boy did I enjoy the attention of the recruiter and intrigue of this opportunity. So, when they asked me what it would take to get me to join them, I threw out a number – never expecting them to agree to it. Whew, not only did they agree, they bested it. Wow, was I on a roll!

The problem was I never considered the OC of the new organization and if it was a "fit". I never questioned if I could be as successful in their organization as I was in my current organization and how culture might weigh into my decision. I remember telling my husband, "how can I turn them down, they asked me what it would take and not only did they meet my request, they beat it". I'd given them my word and how was I going to go back on it? Although I didn't realize it at the time, that was the first test of my personal values and how those values would impact decisions and outcomes for years to come. I'd given my word and I couldn't go back on it – it was a matter of integrity. So, although I had a few prickles of doubt, I pushed them aside and my husband and I prepared to move from Cleveland, Ohio to Nashville, Tennessee.

When I arrived for my first day on the job everything seemed perfect. Employees appeared to be happy and open just as hoped and expected. But soon I would learn that everything was not as it seemed. You see, this division was created in what they liked to call a "reverse acquisition".

Top leaders would tell me over and over again, "…that's how the parent company does things, but we don't do it that way here. You see they bought us for a reason. They realized their model was costing too much money and they bought us because we're lean and mean. They want to learn from what we've done and change their model to be more like ours." Prickle, prickle, prickle, that seed of doubt as to whether this was a good culture fit was growing and I was worried I'd made a mistake. No, that wasn't possible, they said all the right things, they had beautiful posters throughout the organization about their values and philosophies and they had a long history of actions that demonstrated their values – no wait, that wasn't this new division – that was the parent company.

Ensuring a proper culture fit is as important to the individual employee and their career as it is to the success of an organization. Not only did I make a huge mistake leaving a company where I fit like a glove and risk damaging my credibility and career, it cost my new employer a huge amount of money in terms of salary, bonus, relocation, training, and the list goes on. Because my values and philosophies didn't match theirs, my actions were contradictory to what they valued and rewarded causing missteps in decision making and relationship building that was critical to our mutual success. Sure I attempted to fake it for a short period of time, but I quickly realized I was miserable and so were they and nothing short of me leaving was going to rectify the situation, and all because I was enamored with the company's name, their brand, their image, and their offer. Never did I consider the importance of their OC and the impact it would have for both my success and theirs.

Building a Strong Organizational Culture (OC)

The importance and impact of OC can't be overemphasized. It's the "secret sauce" of your competitive advantage both internal in attracting and retaining top talent and externally with providing uncompromising service to your customers, but few leaders have the vision and tenacity to grasp it as an integral part of their overall strategic business plan.

What do you think your reaction would be if I told you I had the equivalent of the next iPod©, Post-It Note© or even the next Google© in your industry and that, if implemented, revenue and profits were expected to be triple that of your current products or services? All I can say is WOW – I'd like a piece of that action! And, like me, you'd probably immediately begin looking for ways to capitalize on it and integrate it into your strategic business model. Why is it then that highly competent, seasoned leaders constantly overlook the power of an intentional organizational culture (OC) when developing and implementing their overall business strategy? Quite often it's because it seems much easier to develop new products or services than to deal with those dreaded "people" issues. As a matter of fact, most leaders hire people and then forget about them unless, of course, they do something so egregious they need to be fired – and even then they assume that HR or someone else will handle that too.

But there is a growing body of evidence, which we will discuss in greater detail in Chapter 4 that suggests an intentional OC improves engagement, translating into better results and higher profits. So, as you'll see, "fit" matters and can absolutely be measured and harnessed to create a true, sustainable, competitive advantage that distinguishes your organization from everyone else.

The OC Equation™ – A First Look

As we begin examining **The OC Equation™** consider the following, too common real life conversation many of us have had with colleagues. You recently talked to a friend, colleague, family member, etc. who's just been told he or she is being let go, laid-off, reassigned or maybe, and often more likely, they're just ignored because they don't "fit" in. No matter how the news is delivered, it always comes as a shock followed by the 7 stages of grief – shock, denial, pain, guilt, anger, bargaining, and depression. But once they begin processing the situation, they begin to recognize the long ignored signs and symptoms facing them all along

– they simply didn't "fit" in.

They become acutely aware of that nagging voice inside that kept telling them something was wrong but was ultimately ignored. Although they knew something was wrong, they couldn't quite put their finger on what it was or how to fix it. They recall meetings where they were ignored when they attempted to contribute, they recall being passed over for assignments or promotions even though they had excellent performance ratings, having their ideas and suggestions dismissed during planning sessions, or even being overlooked for the occasional lunch get together. No matter how hard they tried, they just couldn't get any traction as part of the team. Don't get me wrong, no one was ever openly unkind to them directly – they just didn't seem to be embraced and valued as a colleague, team member, leader, etc. and no matter how hard they tried they just didn't fit in.

The reality is it's not because they weren't a good person or they weren't talented. Nope, more likely it's because their values and philosophies didn't align with the organization's values and philosophies and therefore their actions never really "fit" in and generated the response or recognition anticipated. They didn't mesh with the team, which upon closer inspection and personal reflection was because their way of doing things didn't mesh with how the organization did things, creating an uncomfortable environment resulting in mutual stress and ultimately a lack of trust. This lack of trust then further eroded their ability to build and maintain relationships and get results. In other words, the way they did things didn't fit with the organization's norms about how things get done and/or they didn't subscribe to the shared beliefs, values, traditions and behaviors expected by the organization.

If this has never actually happened to you, it's likely you've seen it happen to someone else. That's why, you don't need to speak Harvard to positively impact your OC, engage employees and drive higher levels of performance using **The OC Equation™** which simply states:

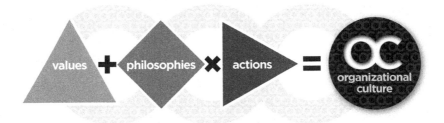

Or as a formula: V + P X A = OC

Even if you try to ignore your organization's OC (and hope it goes away, which most of us do), you and your employees know when it's a fit. You can literally "feel" it. As noted in Chapter 1, you can't escape the OC of the environment you're in any more than you can escape the culture of another country you're in. The OC of an organization is who they are – it's their organizational DNA and it defines how the organization works, how decisions are made, what gets rewarded and even what actions and decisions will get someone fired. The OC encompasses the shared values, beliefs, symbols, and behaviors of an organization. In other words, it's how things get done. It guides both individual and team decisions and actions at a conscious and an unconscious level; and these actions can have a dramatic effect on your company's well-being and success or lack thereof. On an emotional level most employees understand that every organization (be it a business, a department, a non-profit, a boy scout troop, a civic organization or any other grouping of people) has unwritten norms for how things get done but very few can explain how the OC was created or how it's maintained. They just know it when they "see" or "feel" it.

An organization's values set the tone for the company's culture, and they identify what the organization, as a whole, cares about. It's important that employees' values align with your organizational values. When they do, people understand one another, everyone does the right things for the right reasons, and this common purpose and understanding helps people build great working relationships. Now don't misunderstand, creating a unifying OC where employees and leaders share values, philosophies, beliefs and engage in predictable actions does NOT mean hiring people who all think alike and de-valuing diversity. On the contrary, an OC that values diversity will always value diversity and one that doesn't never will until the values, philosophies and actions change. When people work together, share and align their values not only with the organization achieve its core purpose and mission, but individuals will realize their maximum potential and perform at uncommon levels.

On the other hand, when values are out of alignment, people become siloed and work towards different goals. They have different intentions, and achieve different outcomes. Segregating the workforce can damage work relationships, productivity, job satisfaction, and creative potential and ultimately it will create a culture "misfit".

The OC Equation™ - What Does it All Mean?

As previously noted, **The OC Equation™** isn't designed to be complicated.

Applying Gandhi's philosophy to **The OC Equation™** we find: "Your beliefs [Values] become your thoughts [Philosophies]. Your thoughts become your words. Your words become your actions. Your actions become your habits [Organizational Culture (OC)]. Your habits become your values. Your values become your destiny."

The biggest challenge most people have is actually identifying what it is they truly value and then mustering the confidence, courage, and stamina to consistently apply those values to their decisions and actions. To help you understand how simple, yet impactful your OC is, let's explore each of these elements in detail.

The Evolution of Organizational Values

Remember the 1980's and 1990's? Those were years of unprecedented growth and prosperity. During that time it became fashionable for organizations to develop and publish their core values. Many organizations went to great lengths, and expense, to "advertise" the virtuous nature of their enterprises through their published values. They hoped by publishing their values they would strike a chord with the global psyche of consumers giving them a leg up on their competition. Of course, there is a difference between publishing "espoused values" and actually living them. And just because you publish them, doesn't mean anyone actually understands what they are for and how they are expected to be used, especially as it equates to leveraging OC as a competitive advantage.

Little has changed in today's environment, but today organizations are attempting to appeal to a new generation's shifting values which include meaningful work, saving the planet, diversity, fun, opportunities to collaborate, and freedom to challenge the status quo to name a few. The heart and soul of your OC and **The OC Equation™** is *Values* and I mean actual, "real" values upon which decisions are made.

An organization's core values can be defined as those traits or qualities considered not just worthwhile, but that represent your organization's highest priorities, deeply held beliefs, and core, fundamental driving forces. They define what your organization believes and how you as a leader and an organization want to resonate with and appeal to both internal and external stakeholders.

Values are those fundamental, gut level, non-negotiable beliefs and principles that predicate behavior (actions) and dictate how your organization does business forming the foundation for everything that happens in your workplace and how things get done. Core values set the tone for how decisions are made, what decisions are made, who makes them, how employees (yes, all employees) behave, how leaders act, how employees are treated. In short, an organization's core values dictate what actually gets someone hired, rewarded and even what actions get someone fired. Core values are literally the beginning, middle and end of EVERYTHING your organization does and impacts every aspect of your organization.

It can be as simple as valuing productivity and creating an OC that leverages technology to create efficiency. In this organization their primary mode of communication may be email instead of face-to-face meetings. While another organization who values personal relationships and collaboration, focuses more on face-to-face meetings rather than email or instant messaging to get things done because they want to create and reinforce teams who are deeply involved with one another. While this example may appear, on the surface, to be minor and inconsequential, many of the biggest blow-ups in an organization stem from small issues and challenges related to people interactions. For example, employee's expectations for using email or face-to-face interactions for communication that go unaddressed and continue to simmer until they explode onto the surface. As a matter of fact, I have seen high level executives falter in new assignments simply because they didn't spend face-to-face time with individuals who were used to a culture of personal interaction, relationships and collaboration.

Values often exist implicitly, under the radar of awareness, outside formal organizational processes and create an unwavering and unchanging guide that quite literally dictates *how* things get done. Organizational values might be stated in single words, such as Trust, Empowerment, Innovation, Customer-service, Responsibility, Teamwork, Quality, etc. Or they may be value statements, such as "Recognize people as our greatest asset", "Deliver WOW Through Service", "Supporting team member excellence and happiness", "One Global Network," "Results, first - substance over flash", etc. Check out Chapter 5 for more information on evaluating your core values and a list to help you get started. But regardless of how they're articulated, remember values mean little unless they are actually lived through actions.

Values are inevitably driven by people in power within an organization and that can be through either positional power or personal power. Values are most commonly established by the highest level leader in the organization such as the CEO, Owner, Founder, Executive Director, Pastor, or the most influential person reporting to that leader. Lower level leaders who are respected by their peers can and often do establish and nurture their own values within a smaller segment of the organization such as a Department, Division, Office, Unit, Troop, or Pack establishing a sub-culture within the organization. These sub-cultures have the potential to take over the intended OC if the values of the sub-culture are reinforced and rewarded, making the original OC unrecognizable.

It's important that your employees' values align with your organization's values. When this happens, people understand one another, they understand what it means in your organization to "do the right thing" for the right reasons, and this common purpose and understanding helps people build great working relationships. Values alignment helps your organization achieve its core purpose and mission by ensuring employees are working together toward a common goal. When values are out of alignment, people make decisions based on their individual values which may mean they are working toward different goals and outcomes, have different intentions, and different priorities which can result in a culture "misfit". This can damage working relationships, productivity, job satisfaction, and even creative potential. Even if you can't see the misalignment, you most certainly can "feel" it.

Philosophies

Rotten Philosophies = Rotten Organizations

In the previous section we talked about values and how important they are to OC. Back in the go-go days of the uninhibited, prosperous, anything goes, Michael Douglas "Wall Street" 80's and 90's, some prominent companies, like Enron and WorldCom, were admired for their espoused corporate "values" and groundbreaking business models. The problem is that while they "lived" their values through their actions, those actions didn't match what they claimed to value. Their philosophies, how they "expected" the values to be lived through every day actions, were rotten to the core, built on accounting fraud, lying to regulators, cheating investors, and rewarding insiders who helped perpetuate the fraud to make millions of dollars on the backs of their employees. Employees lost their life savings when the organization crumbled and top executives went to prison.

An organization's philosophies define how their stated values are intended to be demonstrated or "lived" every day. The philosophies establish the expectations for how employees are supposed to act in any given situation. In other words, they bring the stated values to life and ensure they are lived through not only critical decisions and actions, but even the most ordinary, mundane actions. As we saw with Enron and any number of other organizations, an organization's philosophies is the embodiment of its values – the actual values, not what they say they value. As it is with verbal and nonverbal communication, when the two don't mesh, people look to the person's actions for what is true and should be really believed. As a result, if the philosophies aren't clearly articulated and then backed up with consistent actions, the organization will never align with **The OC Equation™** or realize the competitive advantage it offers.

Sustained high performance by employees at all levels can only be achieved when employees commit themselves to the goals of the organization. But that kind of commitment doesn't just happen, it's created when employees, managers, and the company all share certain key values and beliefs about their mutual responsibilities to one another. An organization's philosophies bring those values and shared beliefs to life. They describe your organization's unique OC and define how employees can achieve their full potential within that organization and make exceptional contributions, confident that these will be welcomed and rewarded.

In 2002, the US Congress passed the Sarbanes-Oxley Act (SOX) in response to the Enron, Global Crossing (MCI) and other accounting scandals. The Act was implemented to help protect investors, share-holders and the general public from fraudulent accounting activities and errors by corporations. But the Act went even further by requiring publically traded organizations to develop and implement ongoing, comprehensive ethics programs for all employees. The act, SOX, however, did not provide specific criteria to be included in the training, leaving that responsibility for each organization to decide. That decision continues to force organizations to consider their own values and philosophies as they relate to ethics and then articulate those into actionable items for employees to make ethical decisions.

Case in Point: Aligning Organizational Values, Personal Values and Philosophies with Ethics

When I worked for Eaton Corporation, our values included:

- Make our customers the focus of everything we do.
- Recognize our people as our greatest asset.
- Treat each other with respect.
- Be fair, honest and open.
- Be considerate of the environment and our communities.
- Keep our commitments.
- Strive for excellence.

Our philosophies were purposely built to support these values. As such, when we sought to comply with SOX and implement the prescribed training, we went back to the beginning – the values and philosophies. Then we defined for all employees what ETHICS meant at Eaton.

Business Ethics - Standards of conduct that guide business decisions and actions, based on Eaton's values.
Ethics - Standards of conduct that guide decisions and actions, based on *personal* values.

Eaton articulated their philosophies in specific terms to ensure employees knew how they were expected to embody the Eaton Values through their actions. For example, the philosophy of Ethics under **"Integrity of Recording and Reporting Financial Results"** was described as: "We properly maintain accurate and complete financial and other business records, and communicate full, fair, accurate, timely and understandable financial results. In addition, we recognize that various officers and employees of Eaton must meet these requirements for the content of reports to the U.S. Securities and Exchange Commission, or similar agencies in other countries, and for the content of other public communications made by Eaton."

This level of detail was provided during the training to ensure employees' aligned their actions with the Eaton values and philosophies – not their own. In other words, the expectations were established and clear – we expect you to live the Eaton values by understanding and supporting our philosophies and applying them to our definition of ethical actions. Eaton reiterated their expectations by asking all employees to consider the following questions:

1. Would I be comfortable explaining my actions to my supervisor?
2. Would I feel proud telling my family and friends about my actions?
3. Would I be comfortable if my actions were reported in the news media?

If an organization is to be successful leveraging OC as a competitive advantage, the values and philosophies of the organization must be understood and relentlessly pursued by every employee. Employees' actions in support of the values and philosophies must be encouraged, reinforced and nurtured by every leader every day in every situation. By taking this approach, the philosophies become a holistic belief that every employee and every leader is responsible for upholding the organization's values and philosophies in every given situation regardless of their position or level within the organization.

Actions

In the Enron/World Com example above, their actions, not their espoused values or philosophies, are what spoke volumes about what they truly valued and it's those actions that tell the world how things "really" are, not what you wish they were like.

Actions are the final and most important element of **The OC Equation™**. Actions are an outward demonstration of what your organization truly values, regardless of what you've posted in the lobby or etched in marble in the executive boardroom. Actions ALWAYS speak louder than words. Your actions clearly demonstrate what's important to you as a leader and how you make decisions on what gets someone hired, rewarded and/or fired - period.

Make no mistake, it's not what you wish, hope, or even expect that gets hired, rewarded, reinforced and/or fired. It's what *actually* gets hired, rewarded and fired. A strong, beneficial, game-changing OC is reiterated with every business action taken in your communications, processes, policies, procedures, systems, hiring decisions, firing decisions, bonus awards, commendations, disciplinary actions, meetings, and action planning.

A strong OC is literally reinforced or eroded with every decision that's made. When your actions and decisions align and are consistent with what you purport to value and how you've articulated those values through your philosophies, you demonstrate that you have integrity and you become a role model that others look up to, trust and naturally want to follow. While your organization's values set the tone for your company's culture, and identify what your organization, as a whole, cares about, your actions tell the story of what you really care about.

Demonstrating values and philosophies with actions is much like operant conditioning, also referred to as instrumental learning. What you reward will be repeated. B.F. Skinner, the father of Operant Conditioning, proved that learning occurs through reinforcements and punishments for behavior. When an organization encourages employees to live its values and rewards those actions, employees will repeat them, thus creating how things get done.

Organizational Culture, much like trust, is hard to build but can be destroyed very quickly. OC must be continuously nurtured and protected by constantly asking, "Are the actions of your organization enhancing or destroying the credibility of your values and philosophies?"

It's no accident that in **The OC Equation™** values and philosophies are *multiplied* by actions.

Organizational Culture (OC)

OC is quite simply *how things get done* (the way employees go about their jobs and get results) and is defined and reinforced by the shared values, beliefs, traditions, philosophies and actions of the people who work there. And this is where your organization's true competitive advantage lies – your people and your culture are the only thing your competitors can't duplicate. Think about it, everything, including your products or services, your processes, your systems, your footprint can be duplicated by your competition, but no amount of trying can duplicate your secret sauce - your people and their commitment. Your OC provides you with the means necessary to release your employees' passion, potential and performance.

Organizational Culture (OC) creates the habitat for high employee engagement by creating the conditions needed to meet employee needs, which in turn will ensure those employees are equally committed to meeting the organization's needs.

Case in Point. Recently, while working with a client to introduce total compensation statements to all employees for the first time, a young lady spoke up with pride about the intangible value of the OC at her current employer and the impact that had on her decision to leave a much larger organization (and much larger salary) for her current positon. She shared her personal account that although her previous company paid very well and afforded her lots of opportunities to work on interesting projects and client accounts, she routinely worked 60-70 hours per week and was treated as "just another number". Then she found and connected with the OC at her new employer where she and her co-workers are genuinely engaged in their work, wear many different hats, get opportunities to take risks and are actually "happy". As she explained it, "here the values and philosophies and "culture" aren't just posted on the wall – everyone here really lives them – employees are actually happy to be here."

That's the power of your OC!

The OC Equation™ in Action
1   Every organization has a culture – it's either helping or hindering your success..
2   Building a strong OC takes intentional, disciplined focus.
3   The OC Equation™ provides a simple formula for success..
4   Your organization's actions are governed by your values and supported by your philosophies.
5   Every employee and every leader is responsible for supporting your OC no matter what their role in the organization.

Chapter 4

The Big Why

"Great things are not done by impulse, but by a series of small things brought together." -Vincent Van Gogh

In the first three chapters we outline what organizational culture is and how it's developed through The OC Equation™. Now let's focus on why it's important, why you should care and how an extraordinary vision can catapult your organization to future success.

Why Care About Your OC?

Recently a business colleague said: *"To be perfectly honest, I am ambivalent about this subject [OC] because I feel that most HR people concentrate far too much of their time and effort just talking, and talking, and talking some more about this subject, even though a company's culture is important to recruitment and, most importantly, retention. What line management cannot understand is why HR likes to talk incessantly about culture and other conceptual issues, thereby avoiding the real hard BUSINESS issues that they face every day. While I fully recognize the value of having a well-defined, people-oriented culture, in my view, HR would gain a lot more respect from line management if: a) It would take the time to define the culture of THEIR COMPANY, rather than a "wanna be" culture, b) get management's approval, publish it, and train all management on its content, c) cease all the unnecessary talk about the culture, and d) start to help line management achieve its BUSINESS objectives by utilizing various HR services."*

This comment helped me realize that many business leaders (including HR business leaders) don't fully understand the competitive advantage lying at their fingertips, often untapped and grossly underutilized, waiting to be discovered, harnessed and cultivated as their one true competitive advantage - their OC. So the question becomes – WHY? Why should I give a hoot about this thing called OC (Organizational Culture)? The answer is simple – revenue and profits!

Most leaders, at least the effective ones, make decisions based on data. And for those of you who want to see hard facts and details and take the time to mull them over carefully before jumping into a decision. This chapter will provide you with the validated research needed to link business performance and results to employee engagement and ultimately organizational culture (OC). Simply stated, when employees feel connected to the organization, they become actively engaged, meaning they are willing to expend discretionary effort to make things happen. The Conference Board defines employee engagement as "A heightened emotional and intellectual Connection that an employee has for his/her job, organization, manager or co-workers, that influences him/her to apply additional discretionary effort to his/her work."

Connections are made when employee's feel like they belong and are comfortable with the organization's values and philosophies and how those are expressed through consistent, predictable actions that support those values and philosophies creating the OC.

The Link Between Employee Engagement and Business Results

"A great [organizational] culture (OC) will outperform a mediocre culture," says Dave Logan, author of *Tribal Leadership*. While most of us intuitively accept that an organization's culture (OC) is important, many business leaders dismiss it as a "touchy-feely" management buzz word, not worthy of an active role in the overall business strategic planning process. Now you may be thinking, why are we talking about employee engagement? I thought we were talking about organizational culture (OC). The fact of the matter is that employee engagement, the amount of discretionary effort an employee is willing to exert on behalf of their organization, is a result of the employee's level of engagement.

Through their groundbreaking research, Gallup has repeatedly demonstrated that companies with highly engaged workforces outperform their peers by 147% in earnings per share and realize:

- 41% fewer quality defects
- 48% fewer safety incidents
- 28% less shrinkage
- 65% less turnover (low-turnover organizations)
- 25% less turnover (high-turnover organizations)
- 37% less absenteeism

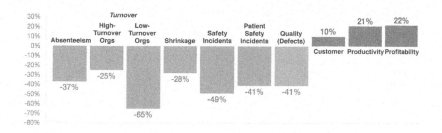

EMPLOYEE ENGAGEMENT AFFECTS KEY BUSINESS OUTCOMES

Work units in the top quartile in employee engagement outperform bottom-quartile units by 10% on customer ratings, 21% in productivity, and 22% in profitability. Work units in the top quartile also saw significantly lower absenteeism (37%), turnover (25% in high-turnover organizations, 65% in low-turnover organizations), and shrinkage (28%) and fewer safety incidents (48%), patient safety incidents (41%), and quality defects (41%).

Source: GALLUP

A highly engaged workforce means the difference between a company that thrives, one that just gets by and one that teeters on the brink of disaster.

A review of prominent research on employee engagement and business performance revealed:

- Engagement does, in fact, equate to dollars. According to Aon Hewitt's 2013 Trends in Global Employee Engagement report, for every 1% increase in employee engagement scores there is an equivalent rise of 0.6% in sales. If this statistic were to be applied to a $5 billion company with a gross of 55% and a 15% operating margin, a 1% increase in engagement would be worth $20 million to the bottom line.
- Towers Watson demonstrated that an OC where communication and change management are highly effective are 2.5 times as likely to be high-performing than those that are not.
- The Temkin Group found that 75% of companies with strong financial results reported high or moderate employee engagement, versus 47% for under-performing companies. They also found that engaged employees work harder than disengaged employees with 96% of highly engaged employees reporting they try their best at work, compared with only 71% of those who are disengaged.

Still skeptical? Kevin Kruse has documented no less than 29 independent research studies that demonstrate a direct correlation between employee engagement and performance. In Kevin's book, *Employee Engagement 2.0*, he describes the documented correlation between engaged employees and business performance using the following graphic:

As you can see from this drawing, culture, that thing that makes employee engagement possible, is critical to recruitment and retention (of both employees and customers) but is also a key business driver of productivity, growth and profit. If business leaders use their OC only at a surface level for recruiting and retention they lose the ability to leverage OC as a long term competitive advantage to achieve extraordinary results. The Hay Group recently reported that employees who are both highly engaged and enabled are 50% more likely to outperform expectations.

And lest you have concerns that these studies are merely a "flash in the pan," studies linking engagement and performance go back for more than 10 years:

- Towers Perrin (2003 & 2005) – engagement levels linked to growth in revenue and operating margin
- Hewitt (2004) – same results as Towers Perrin, but added evidence of "causal link", not just correlation
- Numerous studies link higher engagement to increased salesperson and customer service performance
- Towers Perrin (2003) – engagement strongly linked to employee retention
- Sirota (2004) – engagement linked to increased share price

While these statistics are both compelling and encouraging, merely measuring engagement is not enough to improve results – no Hawthorn effect here! As a leader, you MUST take action to address issues highly correlated with engagement to turn engagement into results. But what actions do you take? The actions you decide on will be largely determined by your organization's values and philosophies which make up your OC.

Towers-Watson took the research a step further in 2011 noting that in addition to engagement, organizations also need to enable and energize employees.

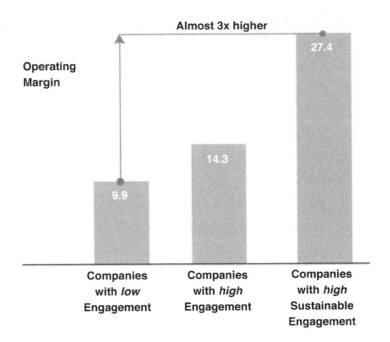

Enabling employees means the OC provides the support employees need to do their jobs effectively and efficiently. They also need to *energize* employees by creating a healthful work environment designed to support employees' physical, social and emotional well-being. In other words, your organizational culture (OC) must address the 6 employee needs discussed in Chapter 6. When employees become frustrated because they do not have the support they need to perform or the work environment doesn't fit their needs, they may be ineffective, even though they are engaged. And if this situation persists, it could lead to attrition or worse – disengagement.

A recent survey by Gallup (October 2013) shows that only 13% of the global workforce is engaged and as many as 63% are "not engaged". In real world terms this means on average only 1 in 8 employees is psychologically committed to their jobs and likely to be making positive contributions to their organizations. The 63% who are considered "not engaged" lack motivation and are less likely to invest discretionary effort in organizational goals and/or outcomes. Another 24% are "actively disengaged" meaning they are unhappy and unproductive at work and likely spend time disengaging their co-workers.

Dismal numbers such as these should have business leaders jumping on the engagement bandwagon. But the report revealed that only 7% of respondent-companies rate themselves highly on measuring, driving and improving engagement and retention and only 12% believe their organizations effectively drive a winning OC.

Further supporting the Deloitte findings is a 2013 Booz & Company study where 84% of the respondents indicated OC was critical to business success but less than half believe their organizations have a winning strategy to do anything about it. While many organizations tout OC as important, only 47% of respondents indicated OC is a priority on a day-to-day basis and considered in leaders' actions. Only 45% of respondents believe OC is effectively managed and leveraged as a strategic advantage. A whopping 96% of respondents say some change in OC is needed and more than half (51%) believe their OC needs a major overhaul.

Changing Workplace Dynamics

It's no surprise, the world is changing and to remain competitive we have to change with it, including considering factors for success that were rarely considered before – such as OC. There are many driving factors for this change including:

- Employees, not employers, are in the driver's seat. In today's marketplace, employees have more information available than ever before – and they use it. Companies such as Linke-dIn, Facebook, and Glassdoor now allow employees to share information about their organization in real time, including job openings, organizational culture, policies, procedures, corporate decisions, missteps etc. Using this information, current employees can quickly infect (positively or negatively) current and future employees.

- Technology is driving new ways to work. The world of work has become increasingly complex. Employees are working more hours each week, but many are working less in the office, connected in remote locations using technology.
- The need for rapid response, agility and flexibility, coupled with heightened technology is changing the way employees work together. The demand for employees to be flexible, continue to learn and develop, embrace empowerment and remain mobile is a driving factor pressuring every organization's OC.
- Employees are no longer motivated by traditional incentives. Today's employees are more focused than ever on making a difference and finding personal and professional purpose in their work. They are committed to finding and working in an environment that reinforces their passions rather than their career ambitions. This trend indicates the need for leaders to focus on the work environment and OC as a competitive advantage.

The majority of today's leaders are Baby Boomers trying to work with employees from four, soon to be five, generations all of whom are motivated by very different things. The one-size fits all approach of yesteryear is no longer a viable option to attract and retain top talent.

Many leaders have never considered their OC, let alone how to leverage it as a competitive advantage. As a matter of fact, many leaders can't articulate their OC, let alone convey it in a meaningful way to others.

This is where the power of your OC really comes into play. The relationship between engagement, enablement and energy is much like a three-legged stool where it takes all three "legs" working in harmony to provide the support necessary to be successful. What's included in those "legs" will depend greatly on your OC which then becomes the "seat" of the stool actually providing the platform needed for the stool to be useful.

What Business Leaders Want

As has always been the case in business, leaders are searching for anything that will give them a competitive advantage in the marketplace. Organizational Culture (OC) is embraced by leaders who recognize it as a sustainable competitive advantage because:

- Today's workforce is looking for more than a paycheck – they want a workplace committed to meeting their needs for belonging, growth, stability, challenge, contribution, and development.
- Following years of accounting scandals in some of the largest and most prestigious companies, such as Enron, WorldCom, and Tyco, organizations are looking to reassure themselves that similar unethical cultures aren't growing in their organizations and regain both employee and consumer trust in the business world.
- In today's competitive, global environment, innovation and high performance are critical to success, but both depend on employee engagement, risk taking, initiative and trust – all of which are reinforced either in a positive or negative way by the OC.
- Organizations need to stay a step ahead of their competition in a way that can't be copied.

In Deloitte's recently released 2015 Capital Trends report, Culture and Engagement was rated by 3,300 global business and HR leaders as the most important overall issue, edging out leadership, which was the leading issue noted in 2014. See the figure below. In addition to noting its importance, the respondents also noted their relative readiness, or lack thereof, to deal with engagement and culture as a strategic initiative.

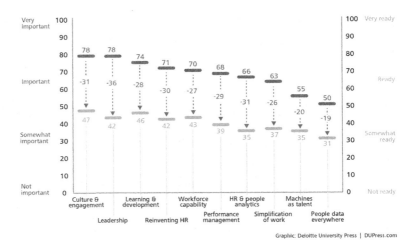

Graphic: Deloitte University Press | DUPress.com

Establishing the OC Needed to Enhance the Bottom Line

As a leader, your greatest contribution to your organization or team is to identify the elements needed for a strong OC and then create the conditions where it can thrive and "live" through employee actions. Your OC reflects the long term health and vitality of your organization. The actions of your employees and your leaders tell the true story of your OC. Whether it's good or bad, whether you nurture it or ignore it, your OC will impact your brand, your employees, your business strategies and your business results, which is why, if supported with intentional actions and leveraged as a business strategy, it can become your one true competitive advantage.

As previously discussed, your OC is simply how things get done in your organization. Behaviors, actions and practices, overt or subtle, which are routinely accepted will drive decision making to achieve the organization's business strategy. To be a sustainable, competitive advantage, your OC needs to be deliberately shaped around **The OC Equation™** - Values + Philosophies x Actions = Organizational Culture (OC) and demonstrated through:

- A compelling purpose.
- A clear, concise, motivating mission and vision.
- Clearly defined and articulated values and philosophies.
- Supporting and reinforcing actions and behaviors that are celebrated, recognized, and rewarded.

An organization that is clear on who they are, what they believe, and how they act will have a competitive advantage because:

- It allows them to attract and retain top talent that are committed to their organizations' strategic goals and objectives and are inspired by the OC to actually engage in the workplace – willing to go above and beyond to achieve results.
- It inspires employees to take responsibility for their actions and be willing to be accountable for decisions because they are supportive of the OC and actively demonstrate the organization's values and philosophies.
- It provides stability in the form of a fixed point of reference for decision making and actions.
- It creates a shared community where employees are connected and enjoy working together.
- It promotes a work environment where employee commitment, dedication and loyalty thrives by creating an emotional connection between employees and the organization.
- It aligns external stakeholders, such as customers and shareholders with the organization's purpose, values and philosophy so they can connect with and articulate what the organization stands for encouraging purchasing decisions based on their own values and philosophies.

Today's workplaces are not known for high levels of commitment and loyalty. That bond was destroyed in the 1980s when organizations began "downsizing" and cutting senior employees with years of service. Although the workplaces of lifelong employment are likely gone forever, both from the perspective of the employer and employee, OC can replace the commitment found in lifelong employment with the commitment of shared values, philosophies and actions.

Blessing White found through their research that organizations with a strong, well-articulated purpose and a long history of living their organizational values, experienced greater employee commitment than employees in organizations with emerging OCs. In addition, their research also demonstrated that more established OCs have less than half as many potentially disengaged or disgruntled employees.

In their ground breaking book, *Corporate Culture and Performance,* Kotter and Heskett revealed that, over a 10 year period organization's that were intentional about living their values and philosophies and managing their OC outperformed their counterparts that did not.

- Job Growth increased 282% vs. 36%
- Revenue increased 682% vs. 166%
- Profit increased 756% vs. 1%
- Stock price increased 901% vs. 74%

In addition to these statistics, the Harvard Business Review noted research indicating that visionary organizations, those with timeless values and purpose, and agile business tactics, outperformed the general stock market and comparable companies in their respective industries. For example, an investment of $1 in 1926 in the New York stock market would have gained $415 by 1990. That same dollar invested in one of the comparison groups would have been worth $955 in 1990. But if that same $1 was invested in one of the visionary organizations with core values, philosophies and a well-defined purpose using agility as a means to remain flexible in their tactical implementation of business processes it would be worth $6,356. While OC is critical to this type of success it is only one of many factors to be considered. Leveraged as a competitive advantage, OC can be the lynchpin for the other factors.

As previously noted, successful leaders make decisions based on facts and data. And in the case of OC, the data are clear – there is a business case to be made for establishing a supportive, positive OC. So strive to be an extraordinary leader by implementing the concepts and principles in this book and demonstrating that you not only understand the importance of a business strategy but you also realize that what drives its success is your OC.

OC and Engagement in Action - OC is More Than a Touchy Feely Buzzword

At Royal Caribbean Cruise Lines, OC is no longer considered a "touchy-feely" buzzword, thanks to Tim Murphy, former CIO. When he took over the IT function, the IT team was considered a bureaucratic silo which did little else but put out IT-related fires. But in 2004 and 2005, through his visionary leadership and attention to OC, the IT department emerged as a strategic partner within RCCL and a key driver of their overall success, landing them on *Computerworld's* list of Best Places to Work in IT.

IT and many other "technical" fields are not usually known for their touchy-feely side, but Tim's visionary leadership understood the importance of connecting with employees, all employees, and meeting not only their extrinsic needs, but their intrinsic needs as well. Connecting with employees through OC is critical to inspiring them to move beyond "just good enough" to extraordinary.

Leading companies have been using "big" data for a number of years now and measure innumerable factors related to performance. But for exceptional organizations, like 3M, they also realize that touchy-feely is what drives big data. At 3M engagement is correlated with innovation, one of their key business drivers. 3M's own internal research found that business groups with more engaged employees were more innovative and produced more products than business groups with low engagement. Their findings also indicate that these increases in innovation resulted in high profitability and lower absenteeism within the business group.

Karen B. Paul, manager of 3M's HR Engagement and Measurement Center stated, "…when it comes to assessing the business outcomes of [employee] engagement initiatives, qualitative outcomes are just as important as quantitative outcomes. Success is when the hallways buzz with energy, when people come to work excited and when they are proud to be associated with your dynamic organization". As we noted before, engagement alone without the OC to support it for the long haul, isn't enough to create a sustainable competitive advantage.

What it Takes to Win

The evidence supporting engagement and OC as an undeniable competitive advantage and their impact on business results is undeniable. Yet many leaders have no idea what OC actually is or how to begin identifying, developing and implementing a positive, winning OC. Their efforts often fail because they try to simply imitate what others are doing without regard to WHY they are doing it, and that won't work. Your OC is individual and personal and derived from your values and philosophies. Don't be fooled into thinking you can simply identify your current OC and then pop a few "perks" in place, such as free lunches, open offices (hotels), telecommuting, or flex-time, to make people happy. This approach will end up costing you money and will have no lasting, appreciable effect on overall engagement or performance. As a matter of fact, your current OC may be hindering, not helping your competitiveness.

Effective leaders need two components to win in the marketplace: (1) A winning strategy and (2) the OC to support it. This is where you and this book can really make a difference. In the chapters to come we will take you through the process of identifying your current OC, articulating your personal and organizational values and philosophies, aligning actions (policies, processes, systems) and measuring results. You're on a journey and like any business strategy there is no quick fix and no final destination, once you achieve one level of commitment and achievement, it's time to raise the bar.

The OC Equation™ in Action
1   Visionary leaders inspire employees by connecting with them and addressing their needs. .
2   OC is more than "touchy-feely", it's a strategy in its own right.
3   Leaders need both a winning strategy and the OC to support it to move from ordinary to extraordinary.

Part 2
Where Is Here?

Chapter 5

You Have to Define Who You Are Before You Can Define What You Want Your Organization to Be

Discovering Your Values - Defining Your Philosophies

Coke, **Zappos,** Southwest Airlines, Disney, Google, Whole Foods, Apple, Nordstrom. When you hear these company names you likely automatically think – "WOW, those are great companies!" However, they didn't get to be great by accident. One thing they all have in common is strong, productive Organizational Cultures (OCs) that drive business results.

When people think about the incredible OCs of these organizations, they think about the tangible, superficial perks, policies and programs they offer. Things like relaxed dress codes, unlimited vacation, free gourmet lunches, "hotels" replacing offices, ping-pong tables for team building, beer Thursdays, parking allowances, and even core values and mission statements. And with the promise of superior results to match theirs, you might be inclined to think, utopia - I'll just copy what they do and use their proven OC in my organization. If only it were that easy! You can't simply copy another organization's OC and expect it to work in your organization or produce the same results – and therein lies the competitive advantage – no one can copy your OC either!

According to Doug Lipp, author of *"Disney U – How Disney University Develops the World's Most engaged, Loyal and Customer-Centric Employees"*:

> *"The Disney University has a set of crystal-clear values that are aligned with and fiercely supported by the company leadership. Many organizations have invested huge sums of money and countless hours studying the Disney way of doing business. They have done an admirable job of analyzing and then mimicking Disney's strategies for creating, building, and opening facilities that have world-class potential. But how successful are those businesses, resorts, hospitals, and organizations (for-profit, as well as not-for-profit) at maintaining what they've created? Many fail in this department for two reasons:*
>
> 1. *They focus on the stuff, the things, without the bedrock of values.*
> 2. *They don't fully consider long-term consequences, the effect of short-sighted decisions on long-term success.*
>
> *Without the conscience of passionately accepted organizational values leading the way, it is far too easy to begin cutting corners. There is a price to pay when things and the bottom line become the main focus. There are no exceptions to this rule."*

Part One – Discovering Your Values

Before you can begin developing your own competitive OC, you must first understand the heartbeat of your OC, which are your organization's values and the importance of those values in driving a competitive OC.

Values are the often untapped powerhouse behind OC because they define the organization's deepest held beliefs and influence employee actions. Values form the basis of how employees are expected to behave, the decisions they will make and the actions they will engage in or reject.

If employees connect with your organizational values they will align their actions with those values and their actions will embody your philosophies. If your culture evolves through the influence of numerous individual values employee actions will often mirror the values and philosophies of the strongest personality in the department or organization hampering optimal alignment that has the power to drive the business strategy.

A competitive OC begins with effective values. For these stated or espoused values to be effective, they must be woven into the very fabric of your organization and ingrained in the organization's DNA. In other words your stated values must be clearly articulated, demonstrated, rewarded, and measured, otherwise, they won't survive. How can you recognize your organization's values? Look at what gets someone hired, fired, or rewarded – that's the best indication of what your organization truly values.

Organizational values, much like personal values, are most evident when the stakes are high, when things go wrong, when it's hard! It's easy to espouse values when things are going well, but your true values are what you do when things are going bad, when it's stressful and you think no one is watching. It's also during these times when your employees have a heightened awareness of your actions and relate those actions back to the values and philosophies.

So, what are values? An excellent definition comes from Bob

McKown, of XMi, who says, "Values are foundational truths that serve as a basis for how your organization operates, performs, how employees conduct themselves and behave within the organization, department, work group, team and those you serve. Values:

- **Guide** the organization by keeping employees on the right track. Employees at all levels of the organization know what the meanings of each value is so they have a clear guide for how they are expected to act and interact in every encounter. They also know the expectations for how they carry out their responsibilities.
- **Guard** the way employees think and every decision they make. Employees know how the organization defines "right", and they know the ramifications of their recommendations and decisions for both themselves and those they serve.
- **Gauge** every action taken by employees. The values allow employees to evaluate where they are and how they are doing. They provide normalcy."

Discovering Your Values

There are two stages to defining values:

1. Defining your personal values.
2. Defining your organizational values.

It's inevitable, a leader's personal values will impact how they act and react in the workplace, or any setting for that matter. As a leader, what you believe and value, will be the primary driver of the beliefs and behaviors of your employees and your overall organization.

Leaders who want to do the right thing, and are trying to be effective, inspirational leaders, often mistakenly believe that if they simply coach people and model the behavior they want, those examples will permeate the organization and drive high performance. But it's not that simple. People will NOT just naturally adapt to your values as a person or an organization and mindlessly follow you. And even if they do, it won't be sustainable if they don't understand WHY you do what you do and why it should be replicated.

So, before we can articulate and develop a strong, effective OC as a competitive advantage, you must first understand what you personally value.

Defining Your Personal Values

Step 1: Tell Your Story. Write your life's story – your first person narrative detailing the major life events that shaped who you are today. These events or milestones were likely significant or life changing, either in a positive or negative way, because they helped shape who you are. Your goal here is to identify 8-10 major life events. During this exercise, take time to consider the following questions:

- When have you felt most alive? What made you feel that way?
- What situations invoke the most intense emotions you've felt, both positively and negatively?
- What stories inspire you?

Step 2: Rate The Significance. For each milestone event outlined in your life story, rate it on a scale of 1-10 signifying how satisfying or positive it was for you. For each negative milestone, rate it (-1) to (-10) representing how negative or unsatisfying it was to you.

Step 3: List Your Values. Now, that you've got those, consider each major milestone and make a list of the values that sustained you through those events. These may be words or phrases, whatever suits you best. What made the positive milestones such a positive experience for you? For negative events, consider the values that were either absent or threatened that made it so negative for you or values that sustained you during that dark time that made a significant difference. Write them down – don't just think about them. It's okay to repeat yourself if you have recurring values that sustained you time after time during these events.

Step 4: Now Go Deeper. In a perfect world, utopia, what values would be essential for you? What are the non-negotiables? Non-negotiables are the values you hold most dear and are willing to lose money, quit your job, or even die to protect. Write those down.

Step 5: Consolidate. Boil your list down to the vital few. Review the complete list of all the values you've identified and select 6-8 that are most important to you. This list might consist of single values that you feel very strongly about or it might consist of values that emerged repeatedly throughout your life. An example might be your religious faith or your integrity.

Step 6: Identifying What's Really Important. Now, considering your consolidated list ask yourself the following:

- What's really important to me about each value?
- Is it a non-negotiable (could I live without it?)
- Can I demonstrate that value even in the face of despair or adversity?

Use these questions to narrow your list further to what you would consider your *Core Values*. Write them down under the heading Core Values. Most people have 5-7 Core Values.

Step 7: Define Each Core Value. Write a short phrase or sentence articulating what each value means to you. This is for you personally so you can be as blunt as you like. For example, if you had Loyalty as a value, you might define it as "putting the team or organization first".

Step 8: Reality Check: Now ask yourself, "Do I actually "live" these values or are they values I aspire to?" If you live these values now, you're ahead of the game. If these are values you aspire to, ask yourself, "What's keeping me from living these values today?" "What barriers do I face?" "What actions do I need to take to remove those barriers?"

Think back to that prickle, prickle, prickle in Chapter 3 where we were discussing the importance of OC "fit" and its impact on your personal and professional success. By carefully identifying your personal core values you get laser focus on what's most important to you in the meaningful relationships of your life. It allows you to evaluate opportunities based on the connection of your core values with the organization's core values, regardless of whom you work for or where you work.

Now that you've sorted out what makes you tick, it's time to look at your organization's values.

Discovering Your Organizational Values

As previously noted, your personal values will naturally permeate your organizational leadership behaviors and actions – it's inevitable, it's who you are, so it will directly impact the decisions you make and the actions you take and drive the organization's OC. The values of an organization's influential leaders permeate the OC of an organization and outweigh the values of customers, employees, vendors, partners, board members, or other stakeholders.

According to Brandon Smith, workplace therapist and founder of The Worksmiths, LLC, 50% of any OC will be a reflection of the leader's personal values.

Because your organization is an extension of you and what's important to you, the values you bring will influence every personal and professional interaction you encounter.

As you begin discovering your organizational values, you'll have to ask yourself some very hard, personal questions and to get the results needed for a firm foundation to build your OC so it can be leveraged as a competitive advantage. Answer those questions as openly and candidly as possible because even if you can't admit it, others know what you value based on your actions, so, if you don't, you're not fooling anyone but yourself.

Step 1: Contemplate. Ask yourself the following key questions.

- "What do I want people to walk away with from interactions with me and the other employees in this organization?"
- "What are the ideal values I would like to instill in my family?"
- "What values am I willing to promote and advocate?"

It may seem silly and unrelated to ask yourself what values you want to instill in your family, but the values that you adhere to in your personal life will likely be the guiding principles or values in your professional life as well.

Step 2: Write It Down. Actually write out your answers to these questions- don't just "think" them. Commit your answers to paper. As you write these down and reread them they will become solidified in your mind and actions.

Step 3: Dig Deeper. "How do I expect things to get done in this organization?" "What do I want my organization to look and feel like?" "How do I want people to interact and behave?" "What behaviors will bring success to this organization?"

Step 4: Turn Your Answers Into Organizational Values. Now, review the answers to each question and identify the values stated in them. What pops out as recurring themes? Congratulations! You've identified the values upon which you want to lead your organization! Now share your version of the organizational values with other leaders in the organization to get their input. This can be done any number of ways. For example, Zappos Email sent the following out to key people (partners, managers and influencers) in 2005 asking for their input:

> "Companies have core values, and we're working on defining them explicitly for Zappos so everyone is on the same page... But the purpose of this email is to ask what everyone's personal values are... please email me 4 or 5 values that you live by (or want to live by) that define who you are or who you want to be... (do not cc everyone)... each value should be one word or at most a short phrase (but ideally one word)... please email me the values that are significant and meaningful to you personally, not necessarily having anything to do with the company's values..."

As you're developing your organizational values, remember they can be single words or phrases. For example, Zappos' values include: *Deliver WOW Through Service* and Hubspot's values include: *We are maniacal about our mission and our metrics.* Some values consist of simple words such as *S-T-A-R-T which stands for: S-Safety, T–Teamwork, A-Accountability, R-Responsiveness and T-Trust.*

Step 5: Write Them Down – Don't just think about them. As with your personal values, don't be concerned if you find you're repeating yourself. That's a good indication the values are organizational core values. Include them on your organization's list of core values.

Step 6: Reality Check: As with your personal values, it's time for a reality check. Ask yourself:

- "Are these *prime* values?"
- "Do they guide "how" I/we expect people to work and conduct

themselves?"

- "Are they a source of distinction?"
- "Are these derived from my/our personal values?"
- "Does each one represent a non-negotiable guiding principle?"
- "If changed, would it alter the character of the organization?"
- "Am I/we committed to living by these values, even when things get tough?"
- "Do I/we actually "live" these values or are they values I aspire to?" If you live these values now, you're ahead of the game. If these are values you aspire to, ask yourself, "Why don't I demonstrate these or live these today?" "What barriers do I face?" "How do I remove those barriers?"

Now that you've identified both your personal and organizational values it's time to consider your goals and objectives for creating a values-based organization.

Step 7: Articulate Your Values as OC Objectives. Begin articulating what you hope to accomplish by leading a values-based organization. To do this, take your organizational values and the answers to your questions in Step 6 and begin formulating some basic statements that outline *how* things are expected to get done in your organization or *how* employees are expected to treat each other. These OC objectives outline the end state your OC should help achieve. Ideally you will have 4-6 OC strategy objectives when you're done.

For example, objectives in your OC strategy might include *"Create an environment where cooperation and teamwork become routine and it becomes a habit that we naturally cooperate and assist each other"* or *"Create an environment where employees are accountable for their commitments and expect that their performance will be measured"*. As you build your OC Objectives refer back to your values (both personal and organizational) to ensure your objectives exemplify the definition associated with each corresponding value.

Step 8: Get Others Involved: Now that you've identified your personal and organizational values and developed your OC strategy objectives, it's time to run them by your leadership team and/or employees. Buy-in is critical to successful deployment and long term sustainability. But don't be surprised if you meet with resistance. Definitions are important and it's likely others will define the values a little differently based on their own personal value systems. Don't be surprised when you throw yours out there if others agree with the value but disagree with your definition. They may be uncomfortable and resist moving in this direction. Some employees, including leaders may even decide to leave the organization if they decide they can't support your value definitions.

Your first OC test! Is your OC important enough to you to risk attrition? If it is, you'll have to let them go, no matter how talented they are. If not, you'll never be able to sustain a long-term, competitive OC.

With that being said, you will need to be flexible about tweaking your definitions and the wording of your OC strategy objectives to gain support and buy-in. But don't sacrifice the true intent of your value definitions. It's important to stay true to yourself as the leader of the organization, while you collaborate to refine the definitions as a team to ensure leaders are prepared to actively demonstrate their commitment to the OC. It's through the team's understanding and support that your values will be supported by philosophies and actions when times are tough and will be sustained even when you're not there.

Part Two - Defining Your Philosophies

Once you've defined your organizational values, it's time to develop and define your organization's philosophies. Ideally you want 6-8 philosophy statements that embody your organizational values. These statements explain how the values are *intended* **to be demonstrated or "lived" by every employee every day and demonstrated through their** decision making.

For example, one of Eaton Corporation's core values is "***Recognize our people as our greatest asset***". They articulate what that value means using the following philosophy statement: "***We expect the best of ourselves and each other***" and back it up with the following definition: "*We believe that employees want to do the right thing for customers, for the company, and for one another. Our workplace policies and decisions are based on that premise. By always doing our best, we constantly validate that belief through our actions.*" Having such a clearly defined philosophy statement makes it easier to keep leaders and employees grounded when questions arise.

Let me demonstrate. Let's go back to our value of recognizing our people as our most valuable asset, and let's say we have a philosophy statement stating, "Compensation is fair and competitive for performance that contributes to the success of the business. It is essential that employees be rewarded both fairly and competitively for their contributions to our success. The greater the contribution the greater the reward."

Then comes the test. In a year of economic turmoil you begin discussing the merit budget with your leadership team and how, or if, you can afford to give employees pay increases. Several ideas get batted around including:

1. Freezing salaries and giving no one an increase this year.
2. Providing an across the board 2% cost of living increase to all employees.
3. Only providing increases to employees who performed at the highest level and contributed significantly to the organization's financial success.

When questions such as these arise, you develop and sustain a competitive advantage through your OC by going back to your values and philosophies to make key decisions based on your guiding principles.

Living your values and philosophies builds trust and loyalty with your employees and establishes the personal connection needed to actively engage employees. **The OC Equation™** helps you build and sustain a positive, winning OC that can be leveraged as a competitive advantage, even when times are tough.

By defining your philosophies you provide laser focus on how success is defined within your organization. How things get done, how employees are expected to behave. Your philosophies tell employees what's important, what should be paid attention to, what should be ignored, what things mean, how to react, how to navigate the political aspects of the organization and even how to behave.

Your philosophies articulate a disciplined, intentional approach toward relationships, interactions, tasks, policies, processes, procedures and responsibilities. They establish standards for behavior and exemplify the characteristics and qualities needed for the organization to be successful.

Articulating your philosophies is difficult but it's worth the effort.

Step 1: Ask.

- What principles or doctrines are needed to ensure the success of this organization?
- What principles or doctrines do we want employees at all levels to use when making decisions that affect themselves, co-workers, their department, the organization, customers, etc.?

Step 2: Review Your Organizational Core Values & Align with Your Philosophies. Go back to the answers you and your team developed to the questions in Step 3 under Defining Organizational Values. Use these as a guide to develop and define your organizational philosophies.

Step 3: Verify. Verify that your philosophy statements support and align with your values and make it very clear how employees are expected to do their jobs, work with one another and conduct themselves. It's critical that your organizational values and philosophy statements complement each another. Contradictions are the kiss of death to a strong, effective, competitive OC because it confuses employees and increases the likelihood that organizational actions by employees and leaders will be independently justified based on the crisis of the moment and each person's personal values.

Step 4: Roll It Out to Others. Once you and your team have gained consensus on both the values and philosophies, it's time to roll them out to all employees. Be sure you include specific examples of how employees should act in various situations and use these documents in their decision making process.

Step 5: Live It Through Your ACTIONS! Values and philosophies are worthless without ACTIONS to back them up. This is where the rubber hits the road and where most organizations fail and OCs fall apart.

Let's take a look at two different organizations whose actions clearly demonstrate what they value and the philosophies they live by and how those actions resulted in very different outcomes.

Enron, the shamed energy, commodities and services, company presumably had carefully crafted values which included **Integrity, Communication, Respect** and **Excellence**. These values were etched in marble in their lobby for all to see, but their leaders' actions went directly against these values ultimately bankrupting the company and landing the top executives in jail. In other words, Integrity, Communication, Respect and Excellence weren't what Enron really valued. Their actions contradicted their values demonstrating what their actual organizational values were. Contrast that with Zappos, the customer service giant, who is so committed to actually living their stated values that they offer new hires $4,000 to leave the company during their orientation period – no strings attached. Their logic? It's cheaper to pay employees $4,000 to quit than it is to risk destroying their competitive advantage – their OC.

Remember, ACTIONS speak louder than words. That's true in communications and in defining your OC.

The OC Equation™ in Action
1   Begin with the end in mind – what OC do you need to engage employees and create a competitive advantage?
2   You cannot separate your leaders' personal values from your organization.
3   Understand how your personal values integrate into your organizational values.
4   Articulate what those values mean by creating philosophies.
5   Remember, ACTIONS speak louder than words!

Chapter 6

The Ultimate Business Strategy– Merging Business with Human Capital Strategies

"Culture Eats Strategy for Lunch" ~ Peter Drucker

It Takes More than Funding and Education to Ensure Success

Where was the first flight invented? Ohioans will tell you Wilbur Wright invented flight at his Dayton, Ohio home. But North Carolinians will tell you he invented it a Kitty Hawk, North Carolina. But did you know that the US government actually subsidized someone else to invent flight?

Dr. Langley, the director of the Smithsonian Institution and one of the most renowned scientists of his day, became interested in flight and was able to marshal tremendous technical and financial resources. In fact, the US federal government gave Dr. Samuel Langley a $70,000 grant to invent the first heavier-than-air flying machine. After receiving the grant, he quickly assembled a dream team of scientists and top minds charged with inventing a heavier than air flying machine.

Contrast that with Wilbur Wright who was very bright and mechanically inclined but who never finished high school or went to college. He and his brother, Orville, were fascinated with machines and passionate about flight and decided to pick up where German aviator Otto Lilienthal left off when he was killed in a glider accident.

Wilbur and Orville took $2,000 from their bicycle shop in Dayton, Ohio and started developing their flyer, working on it in their spare time. They later moved the project to Kitty Hawk, North Carolina in an effort to take advantage of the strong winds on the outer banks and test their invention. There, Wilbur assembled a highly ambitious, dedicated team who were so inspired by his vision they pulled out all the stops to make his vision of flight a reality.

On December 17, 1903, the Wright brothers succeeded in making the first free, controlled flight of a power-driven airplane. It was an extraordinary achievement unmatched by Dr. Langley's government funding or "dream team" of highly educated scientists.

Inspiring Greatness to Achieve Success

Business leaders have a universal goal – to win. But that goal can't be accomplished unless those leaders have two critical elements in their arsenal: (1) a winning business strategy and (2) the organizational culture (OC) required to make it happen.

There are three critical elements to an organization's long-term success:

1. Strong, purposeful, visionary leadership.
2. A winning business strategy.
3. The Organizational Culture (OC) to make it happen.

Most successful businesses develop and implement a business strategy that fits their definition of how to win in their niche marketplace. And while that's a great first step, a strategy is only as good as its execution and that's where their OC comes in.

While **The OC Equation™** (values + philosophies X actions = OC) helps leaders understand what it takes to create and sustain a positive

OC there is no single OC that works in every organization.

Four legendary cultures that create exceptional value for their organizations are identified in a December 19, 2013 article in the Harvard Business Review entitled "The Defining Elements of a Winning Culture" by Michael C. Mankins, AM:

- Kent Thiry built a values-focused culture at DaVita and transformed the company from a laggard to the world's leading provider of kidney dialysis services.
- Alan Mulally created a "working–together" spirit at Ford Motor Company that focused and re-energized the automaker, reversing a decades-long slide in market share.
- Herb Kelleher fostered a culture of employee empowerment and cost containment at Southwest, enabling the airline to become one of the world's most admired and profitable carriers.
- Steve Jobs built a challenging culture at Apple where" reality is suspended" and "anything is possible'" and became the most valuable company on the planet.

And therein lies the reason why your OC IS your competitive advantage. In "Who Says Elephants Can't Dance?" Lou Gerstner put it this way: "Culture isn't just one aspect of the game – it is the game. In the end, an organization is nothing more than the collective capacity of its people to create value."

A strong OC at your organization requires empowering leadership that can articulate a common vision and purpose and inspire employees to accomplish the business objectives and create value through the culture. This is where companies that don't truly understand and value OC as a competitive advantage go astray. They make the mistake of thinking if they simply create a culture where employees "feel good" and are happy, the results will automatically come. But that's not how it works; results take work and commitment. Feeling good, being "satisfied" or "happy" won't necessarily produce results. Ask yourself, "Have I ever seen an employee who was completely 'happy' being 'retired in place'"?

While a strong OC is crucial to the kind of unprecedented success outlined in Chapter 4, it must be aligned with the business strategy to produce extraordinary results. By definition, a winning OC not only expects, but demands, performance and leadership foster an environment where all stakeholders win.

Articulating an inspiring vision and setting the direction of the organization

Leadership

Strategy

Culture

The mission & vision. Conduction a SWOT analysis, developing a buisiness strategy with action plans & objectives.

Distinctive characteristics that ensure the 6 employee needs are met:
1. Stability and certainty
2. Challenge
3. Recognition
4. Belonging
5. Development
6. Contribution
How Things Get Done Around Here

The Role of Leadership

Read any business book and it will tell you that for an organization to prosper it needs strong leaders who establish an inspiring vision that others want to be part of. It's a connection that goes beyond attendance to commitment. It permeates the workplace and manifests itself in the actions, beliefs, values and goals of all employees.

The fundamentals necessary to excite and inspire people to want to follow a leader include:

- Clearly set organizational direction and purpose;
- Involve employees in decisions that affect them;

- Display and reflect the unique values, philosophies, beliefs, strengths and direction of the organization;
- Inspire enthusiasm, loyalty, commitment and excitement in company members;
- Help employees believe that they are part of something bigger than themselves and their daily work;
- Have open, honest, communication that is transparent; and
- Challenge people to outdo themselves, to stretch and reach.

According to Simon Sinek in *Start with Why*, "There are leaders and there are those that lead." He describes leaders as those who are in a position of power or who have a given title while those who lead are able to inspire others to act through a sense of belonging and purpose. In other words, a connection is not only *what* they do, but *why* they do it. Something bigger than themselves. Marcus Luttrell, author of "Lone Survivor", recently spoke to the Alabama Crimson Tide football team stating "being a Navy Seal is not what I do, it's who I am". Inspiring leaders spark something in a person that compels them to follow the leader because they are moved by their compelling vision and purpose.

Inspiring leaders think, act and speak differently from ordinary leaders. They don't simply view the world as a series of goals, objectives and tasks that must be accomplished to succeed. Rather they view the world and what they do from the context of a sense of purpose. They articulate an inspiring vision (a purpose) behind what they do and why they do it and then connect with others that relate to and believe in that purpose.

In his book *Delivering Happiness*, Tony Hsieh, CEO of ZAPPOs, discusses his decision to leave his first job at Oracle where he was a software engineer because he was bored and felt unfulfilled. Ultimately his dissatisfaction and lack of engagement was the result of a boss who told him what to do (the tasks to be completed), rather than why he should do it (why his work had purpose and meaning). His boss wasn't a leader who could inspire him to use his talents to achieve a higher level of compelling vision. It takes great leaders to inspire ordinary employees to deliver great performance and create great companies.

A Winning Business Strategy

In the 1980s and 1990s it became quite fashionable for companies to develop mission and vision statements for their organization. These statements were supposed to help the organization articulate the reason for their existence so every employee understood the company's direction and could see how their jobs fit into the bigger picture. Supporting the vision and mission was the business strategy that described the goals, objectives and tasks that needed to be accomplished by employees to ensure the company's success.

It was a lofty idea with good intentions that was doomed to failure. Most mission and vision statements overflowed with flowery, pompous language that was impossible to understand or connect with as an employee or customer. The neatly framed statements often hung in corporate board rooms or were posted on the company website never to be read again. Unfortunately that short sightedness resulted in a missed opportunity to engage employees in the *purpose* behind their organization's products or services. In other words, they failed to help employees connect to the organization's reason for existence in a meaningful way that would instill pride, a sense of belonging and the will to take action to ensure its success.

Now don't get me wrong, I am not saying that vision and mission statements aren't valuable. On the contrary, well written, simple, concise and inspiring mission and vision statements can help employees and customers connect with the company. For example, Apple's vision is to "Challenge the status quo, constantly innovate and be simple rather than complex". Whole Foods' vision reaches beyond food sales stating its ..."deepest purpose as an organization is helping support the health, well-being, and healing of both people — customers, Team Members, and business organizations in general — and the planet". As you can see these companies' visions go well beyond their product – they look to connect people with their purpose and build a following based on that purpose. Your organization can do the same, if your OC embraces and reinforces strong, purposeful, visionary leadership.

A Case Study in Leadership and Purpose

Still not sure the power of a leader's compelling vision? Consider the unprecedented uncertainty of the American Revolution and the leaders of that war. If America prevailed we would launch an independent nation free of British oppression, but also free of British money and protection. If we failed, our best and brightest leaders and their followers would be tried for treason and hanged. Talk about high stakes and uncertainty!

So, how does an inspirational, purpose-driven leader lead during times when not only is the business strategy is at stake, but people's very lives and livelihoods are at stake? Let's look to the Father of our country, George Washington, for insight.

On December 25, 1776, George Washington led his troops to a substantial victory over the British Redcoats at Trenton, NJ. This victory was considered a turning point in the Revolutionary War and put the U.S. on track for victory. But it was an impending victory that his troops couldn't quite see or appreciate considering the ravages of war and the extreme conditions facing his troops (it's that forest for the trees thing).

At this pivotal moment in history, Washington's troops were freezing in the severe winter weather and only a smattering of the original troops remained. Many soldiers simply deserted seeking to return home as they were consumed by their perceived hopelessness for the cause. Those that remained were loyal, they had fought gallantly at Breeder's Hill, White Plains, Kip's Bay and other locations and they remained steadfastly committed to the cause. But they also had a personal decision looming. Under the conscription laws of the times, their enlistment would expire on January 1, 1777 and most, if not all of them, had decided they would not continue. Rather they would return home to their families and try to put their lives back together, giving up the dream of freedom. This was an easy and honorable way out of what most thought was a lost cause. Just as Washington was on the brink of turning the tide and victory was at hand, his troops had decided they'd had enough and would not continue. The revolution was lost.

Faced with this reality, Washington gathered his remaining troops at Assunpink Creek for one last meeting. His troops were not fighting men by nature; they were farmers, laborers, and tradesmen, family men with families to consider. So, he decided to make them an offer they couldn't refuse – he offered them a $10 bonus if they would remain for a few more months. While that may seem minimal by today's standards, it was a hefty sum in 1776 and its significance didn't fall on deaf ears. Every man there understood Washington's confidence in offering them such a large sum. With all the fanfare of a drum roll, Washington asked for anyone interested in the bonus to step forward. And he waited and waited, but no one stepped up. Not a single taker! Distraught, Washington galloped off on his horse, but his men didn't break formation. They stayed in place on the cold, windy hill – waiting…

One of those men was Nathaneal Greene who detailed in a letter sent to Nicholas Cooke the events of that day. You see, General Washington returned to his men after reconsidering his position and his leadership. He returned literally with his hat in hand. Gone was his arrogance and overconfidence. This time he talked with his men, not at them, with both affection and gratitude, saying the following: "My brave fellows, you have done all I asked you to do and more than could be reasonably expected, but your country is at stake, your wives, your houses, and all that you hold dear. You have worn yourselves out with fatigues and hardships, but we know not how to spare you. If you will consent to stay one month longer, you will render that service to the cause of liberty, and to your country, which you can probably never do under any other circumstances." He spoke from the heart and reminded his men of their higher purpose. He told his men that he too wished the burden of war and the birth of a nation could be passed to others, but there was no one else, just them. He implored his men to consider what they alone could achieve, asking them to think not only of themselves, but the greater good of their fellow countrymen and their country, promising that if they would stay and fight they would change the world. With the inspiring vision and purpose clearly laid out, he asked once again for takers to step forward. Seconds seemed like minutes, but finally the first follower stepped forward breaking the dam and giving others the courage and fortitude to step forward as well. In the end, every man stepped up and recommitted themselves to the vision, mission and more importantly the purpose of a budding nation. They were well on their way to achieving that vision and turning their simple little cause into a reality that would literally change the world.

What Washington discovered on that snow covered hill was that people are inspired to greatness and commitment not by perks and money, but by a compelling vision with the opportunity to belong and rally around a defined purpose.

This seems so simple, but few leaders figure it out, missing an opportunity to unleash the passion, potential and performance of employees to achieve what seems to be impossible. Because of our own lack of confidence and passion, we often fail to establish a common, compelling vision and purpose for our organization. Without a unifying purpose, silos are established, personal agendas emerge and anarchy reins because people do what people do – they unilaterally decide what's important to them and in their best interests establishing and literally creating a "culture within a culture".

When we're talking about developing an organizational culture that supports and enhances your competitive business position, competing agendas and personal goals and objectives pit employees and departments against each other creating rivalries and silos in a dog eat dog world resulting in a negative culture where it's every employee for themselves, limiting the effectiveness of all resources and creating insurmountable obstacles to organizational success.

Connecting Business Needs with Employee Needs

Studies show over 80% of Americans say they don't have their dream job. If more leaders knew how to inspire and create the conditions for a great OC, they could connect in such a way as to reverse that statistic. One where employees are passionate about their organization, their job and going to work.

We've all heard the adage "employees don't quit companies, they quit leaders". While that is certainly a true statement, contrary to popular belief, employees also don't join your organization and stay because of WHAT you do (your products and services). They come because of WHY you do it – the organization's purpose and how that purpose fulfills their needs. This has never been more important than it is now with the emerging millennial generation, who, more than their predecessors make decisions based on those connections.

All employees, regardless of their role in the organization, have 6 basic needs:

1. Stability and Certainty – to know if they perform there will be opportunities.
2. Challenge – to be stimulated by the work they do and not to be bored.
3. Recognition – to feel appreciated for the work they do.
4. Belonging- to feel part of something bigger than themselves.
5. Develop – to grow and learn.
6. Contribution – to feel their work makes a difference.

Strong, purposeful, visionary leaders create an OC that connects employees to the organization in a way that fulfills these needs while subsequently meeting the needs of the organization. Meeting employee needs is important because employees who are passionate about going to work and what they do are more productive and creative, they arrive at work more engaged, they go home more content, they have happier families, and they treat their co-workers and customers better. Their passion and performance enhance company performance making strong companies and strong economies.

Like George Washington on that windy hill, these leaders clearly communicate an inspiring and compelling purpose and connect people to their vision and mission in a way that makes achieving it seem possible; super charging their employees to invest their mind, body and soul into achieving greatness. But what is a mission and vision and why is it important?

Visions are nothing more than a statement of the leader's desired future. They're big, bold declarations of the leader's dream for the organization and how its products and services will positively impact the world. Visions are meant to inspire, energize, and create a captivating picture of the organization and its future. As mentioned earlier, a vision statement must be easily understood and employees must be able to connect to it on a personal level. Keeping those goals in mind, let's look at how to create an effective vision statement.

Your vision statement answers the following question:

Why does my organization exist and where is it going?

Top Five Things to Keep in Mind When Writing Your Vision Statement

1. Describe your desired future – think outcomes that are five to ten years out.
2. Dream big and focus on your definition of success.
3. Write your vision statement in the present tense.
4. Infuse your vision statement with passion.
5. Paint a graphic mental picture of the organization you want.

Remember, your vision sets the tone for your organization and its culture. It defines its purpose and gives employees something to connect with immediately and in the future. It should inspire, energize, and motivate. Above all else it must describe what will be achieved if your organization is successful. It is impossible to plan the direction of your organization without one. Follow these guidelines, and use the vision statement formula to perfectly articulate your dream, your passion, and the direction you envision for your business.

Articulating a Compelling Vision

Think back to when you first dreamed of starting (or joining) your organization. Remember that giddy exuberance for what you were trying to accomplish and capture what excited and engaged you. Those same elements will connect your employees and your customers. Dare to dream BIG. Answering the following questions will help you to create a verbal picture of your organization's purpose:

- *Why does your organization exist?* What do you want for yourself, your family and your customers? Think about the spark that ignited your decision to start the organization. What will keep it burning?

- *Who are your customers?* What can you do for them that will enrich their lives and contribute to their success--now and in the future?

- *What image of your business do you want to convey?* Customers, suppliers, employees and the public will all have perceptions of your company. How will you create the desired picture?

- *What underlying philosophies or values guided your responses to the previous questions?* Some organizations choose to list these separately. Writing them down clarifies the "why" behind your vision.

Answer the questions above, but keep it simple to inspire, engage and connect others.

The purpose of my organization is to_____

_____. (How does it change the world and make it and everyone in it better?)

For example, the purpose behind Dave Ramsey's LAMPO Group is to change lives and give people hope. To help them believe they can be financially independent and free from debt in the future. Because of this stated purpose, every employee is inspired by the part they play in delivering that hope to people. They connect their job, whether they are in development, IT, shipping, or customer service with giving others HOPE. This purpose transcends the products they sell, it connects, engages and inspires.

If your organization already has a vision statement, is it big and bold? Does it inspire, does it connect people and engage them to go above and beyond to make it happen? Is it relevant to changing demographics among customers, employees and other stakeholders? If not, what needs to be changed to address these issues?

Here are a few inspiring visions from companies you know:

- To make the world's information universally accessible and useful - **Google**
- To inspire and nurture the human spirit – one person, one cup, and one neighborhood at a time - **Starbucks**
- Be our customers' favorite place and way to eat - **McDonalds**

Sixteen years later, Google is reconsidering its original vision crafted in 1998. When questioned by the newspaper *Financial Times* as to whether Google needs to alter its vision, which was intertwined with the company mantra "don't be evil", CEO Larry Page responded: "We're in a bit of uncharted territory. We're trying to figure it out. How do we use all these resources … and have a much more positive impact on the world?"

It isn't hard to write a vision statement. But it is sometimes difficult to write a vision statement that truly encapsulates the purpose behind your organization. When you write your vision statement, make sure that you articulate what's truly important to you and your organization, that which inspires and energizes you as a leader and then tie it back to your organizational values and philosophies. In terms of **The OC Equation™** an organization's vision (purpose) is an extension of its values. If you don't fully believe in your vision statement, you won't fully commit to it and neither will your employees, customers or other stakeholders.

The Mission Statement

Now that you have an inspiring vision statement, it's time to clearly articulate your organization's mission in a "formal" mission statement. A mission statement is an outward commitment made to achieving the vision through specific actions. It captures, in a few succinct sentences, the essence of the organization's goals and the underlying philosophies that support it. The mission statement encapsulates the underlying philosophies behind the organizational values and sets the stage for actions and decisions that demonstrate the commitment to both the vision and mission.

The mission statement provides a general outline of how the organization will achieve its vision, outlining:

- What the company does,
- How it will do it, and
- Who the company's customers are.

When preparing to write an effective mission statement, consider the following questions:

- *What is the nature of your products and services?* What factors determine pricing and quality? Consider how these relate to the reasons for your business›s existence. How will all this change over time?

- *What level of service do you provide?* Most companies believe they offer "the best service available," but do your customers agree? Don't be vague; define what makes your service so extraordinary.

- *What roles do you and your employees play?* Wise captains develop a leadership style that challenges and recognizes the accomplishments of employees.

- *What kind of relationships will you maintain with suppliers?* Every business is in partnership with its suppliers. When you succeed, so do they.

- *How do you differ from your competitors?* Many entrepreneurs forget they are pursuing the same dollars as their competitors. What do you do better, cheaper or faster than other competitors? How can you use competitors' weaknesses to your advantage?

- *How will you use technology, capital, processes, products and services to reach your goals?* A description of your strategy will keep your energies focused on your goals.

Developing and Implementing a Strategic Plan

Engaging and inspiring employees is only the first step. Once you connect with them and connect them with the organization's vision it's time to lay out a roadmap for how you'll get there. This is where the strategic planning process comes into play.

Strategic Planning is a systematic process designed to help the organization focus on *HOW* it will succeed in the future. During the strategic planning process, an organization committed to using their OC as a competitive advantage not only focuses on specific actions to be taken to achieve the strategic plan but also how the organizational values and philosophies will be demonstrated through those actions so as to reinforce the OC and engage and inspire employees, clients and stakeholders.

Organizational culture and organizational strategy must be intertwined. If your culture doesn't align with and support strategy, your strategy will fail. The OC provides the organization's foundation and framework, while the strategy provides the path to achieve success. If your OC doesn't support your business strategy, your resources and efforts will be fragmented. Your strategy cannot succeed if it is not supported by an OC that provides it with the passion, commitment and effort needed for execution. This is where many organizations fail. They establish a business strategy but fail to align it with an OC that can nurture its realization. Together strategy and culture provide an organization with the only true competitive advantage that can't be duplicated.

Consider Whole Food Markets' "Values Matter" strategy. For centuries, many consumers considered food as a simple necessity to sustain life and in their view all food was created equal. Few gave any thought to where their food came from, how it was farmed, if those farmers received a fair, living wage, or if the products themselves were treated in a humane way.

Whole Food Markets capitalized on the socially conscious consumer of today by devising a business strategy that links the necessity of food with their values and philosophies, purpose and passion of health, sustainability and fair trade. This linkage ensures they "live" their values through their actions and creates an organizational culture (OC) that inspires and engages both employees and customers and prompts them to make personal decisions based on their shared values and philosophies.

In addition to inspiring followers, whether those are employees or customers, great leaders must also understand the importance of a great OC, one that supports employee needs, reinforces the organization's values and philosophies through its actions and inspires and promotes the best in people. Leaders who understand and embrace OC have a competitive advantage that improves both employee engagement and business results.

As a leader, it's your job to create the conditions where your OC can thrive.

As Wilbur and Orville Wright's pathway to flight demonstrated, strategy and a business plan are critical to success, but it's passion about our work that makes us better people. The flames of passion are fanned by effective leaders who engage all employees in the OC by communicating the organizational values and philosophies along with a clear, compelling vision and mission then aligning that with the strategic business plan for future success. By following the principles outlined through **The OC Equation™** you and your organization can also achieve uncompromising business success and build an organization where trust, loyalty and performance are the norm.

Organizational Culture (OC) creates the environment in which your strategy, your brand and your organization either thrives or dies a slow painful death.

But these things don't happen by accident. They must be carefully planned, bought or grown and nurtured. To be successful, every organization needs direction. Like your product or marketing strategy needs direction, your people strategy needs direction too. By using **The OC Equation™** you can develop and articulate the foundation of your people strategy and unleash your employees' passion, potential and performance.

The OC Equation™ in Action

1	Define your passion – why does your organization exist?
2	Establish a clear, compelling vision that rallies employees and customers.
3	Engage and inspire employees by aligning the 6 employee needs with the shared purpose of the company.
4	Ensure leaders demonstrate commitment to the values & philosophies through their actions.
5	Align goals, objectives and expectations to the OC, the strategic plan and measurable business results.

Chapter 7

Assessing and Defining Your OC

Being part of something great

"Walking through the doors of Upshot every day and
feeling the positive mojo that our great culture and happy,
engaged people generate motivates me the most. You
feel it immediately, that sense of something exceptional
happening here. That's a great feeling that I want to perpetuate. I also believe that being a great place to work is
the difference between being a good company and a great
company. When a company truly cares about its people,
nurtures the culture, defines the purpose, creates a great
environment and offers challenging work, great things
happen. Striving to be a great place to work is not easy,
but it's definitely worth it." --
Brian Kristofek, president & CEO, Upshot

Culture can make the difference between a good company and a great company. If you're still not convinced culture is a differentiator, your employees are. A recent study by Booz & Co. found 84% of respondents rated OC as critical to the long term success of their organization, but believed their company does a poor job managing it. Sixty percent of respondents in the survey see culture as a bigger success factor than either the organization's strategy or their operating model.

So, should you consider enhancing your OC as part of your overall business strategy to engage employees and enhance the bottom line? Few organizations would make sweeping changes to their business strategy, product mix, manufacturing processes or service offerings without careful consideration and analysis. Changes to your organizational culture (OC) should be no different. Before jumping on the bandwagon with no clear direction, consider your organization for a moment.

- Do you routinely lose key talent?
- Do employees seem stressed and unhappy?
- Are department or functional silos preventing employees from uniting around a common set of values, philosophies, purpose and vision?
- Is the organization losing focus or commitment as it grows?
- Have you experienced turnover in key positions?
- Are you facing a merger or acquisition that may bring in new leadership, new ideas and new values?
- Does your strategic planning include a culture evaluation and how culture impacts achievement of the strategy?
- Is change needed, but no one knows how to make it stick?

Your organization can prepare itself for long-term success with a carefully crafted and nurtured OC. But beware: your actions must consistently and directly connect with your organization's values and philosophies if a winning OC is to be developed and sustained.

Success comes from building an OC that aligns your organization's values and philosophies through your actions. In other words, live by **The OC Equation™**. By grounding your organization in these principles and aligning your actions to these principles you engage employees unleashing their passion, commitment and performance.

Know Thy OC

Recently a client engaged us to help them develop a proactive culture where employees anticipate current/future events and take the initiative to adapt their actions and/or to shape their results. As we evaluated their current culture we found that the knights in shining armor who swooped in and saved the day were the ones rewarded. It didn't take long for employees to figure out that saving the day was valued more than trudging away in the trenches to avoid crises. Because reactive behaviors were rewarded, employees were perpetually in crisis management mode jumping from one crisis to another and never taking time to plan or develop a strategy.

Meanwhile employees who worked quietly behind the scenes to anticipate obstacles and prevent failure were rarely recognized. Their efforts to prevent crises or save money while protecting clients were ignored and they were viewed as only average performers with little star potential. As a result, these employees only received "average" rewards (merit increases and promotions), while their more reactive counterparts were heralded as heroes, often receiving above average merit increases, hefty promotions and BIG annual bonuses. Is it any wonder their culture was reactive?

Before you can intentionally leverage OC as a competitive advantage, you have to fully understand the state of your current OC and if it is helping or hindering your organization's ability to achieve long term business results. Conducting an OC assessment is vital to identifying the current state and building action plans to close the gap between the current state and your long-term desired state.

Identifying the Current State

There are a number of options that can be employed when conducting an OC assessment, including individual one-on-one interviews, focus group meetings, or by distributing anonymous open or closed ended surveys to employees, former employees and other stakeholders at all levels. Consider if internal employees should be used to conduct these interviews or meetings and gather the surveys or if an external consultant should be used.

No matter what method you choose, the goal is to collect open, honest feedback from a variety of sources covering all levels of the organization. To ensure employees provide reliable information on what's really going on, as opposed to what they think you want to hear, you will have to protect the confidentiality of their responses. Participants must be assured nothing they say will be directly attributable to them and that none of their comments will be used against them. If they are skeptical or hesitant to participate, that already tells you something about the state of your current culture.

Discovering Your Current Culture: A Step-by-Step Process

During a visit to the NASA space center in 1962, President Kennedy noticed a man in the hallway, who was obviously the janitor, carrying a broom. He interrupted his tour, walked over to the man and said, "Hi, I'm Jack Kennedy. What are you doing?"

"Well, Mr. President" the janitor responded, "I'm helping put a man on the moon."

Now, whether this story is true or not doesn't really matter because it exemplifies the general sentiment shared by every employee at NASA at that time. Regardless of how large or visible their contribution was, they all felt a genuine and direct connection between the work they did and Neil Armstrong's ability to step on the moon.

In many ways, the prevalent feeling of being connected to a shared purpose and actively contributing to the Apollo space program was as noteworthy and admirable as the collective feat of sending men to walk on the moon. Although he was "just a janitor", the purpose of NASA was so entrenched in his psyche that he believed his role was vital to the organization's success – and truly it was. Even though each positon contributes to the organization's success in a different way, every position is critical to accomplishing the strategic objectives. If employees don't connect their role to the organization's purpose, they never become fully engaged and committed to its success.

Making this connection doesn't just happen by accident. In fact, if left to individual employees, they may never see the bigger picture of their value to the success of the organization and may never become an integral part of the OC.

Before you decide to change your culture, you must first know what it is. That process begins with a culture assessment. The following step-by-step process will help you discover what your current culture is based on actual versus espoused values, philosophies and actions. This process will also help you articulate the purpose of your organization so you can (1) clearly communicate a compelling vision and mission, (2) establish a meaningful direction, (3) outline specific action plans to achieve the business strategy while inspiring and engaging employees and (4) create a competitive advantage in the marketplace.

Step 1: Identify your current culture by asking questions to discover what your actions, not your words, say about what's really valued and important. In other words, where does your organization "spend" its resources – its people, assignments, time, effort and money? How does your organization decide who gets hired, what gets rewarded, and what leads to someone being fired?

This process begins with a review of your current marketing collateral or stakeholder communications, including employee handbooks, marketing materials, website information, annual reports, memos, meeting minutes, posters, etc. Consider organizational decisions such as:

- What do we "say" we value? Look at both what is physically said and what is written in memos, handbooks, marketing materials, etc.?

- What actions have we taken in the recent past and what do our actions say about what we value? Don't list what you wish your actions demonstrated, list what you actually demonstrated along with concrete examples of situations that demonstrated that.
- Who has been hired, fired or promoted in the past few years? Why were those decisions made?
- How is your organization structured? What policies and procedures are in place?
- What image does your organization portray through its offices, dress code, logo, symbols, marketing, public relations, advertising, and community involvement?
- Does your organization follow formal policies and procedures or are vague guidelines the norm?
- Are employees treated like family and encouraged to share a lot of themselves?
- What's the management style of your organization? Participative, Innovative, Competitive, Conforming?
- What common rallying points exist that bind your employees together – loyalty/trust, innovation, accomplishment/achievement, formal rules and policies?
- What do your leaders emphasize – employee development, taking on challenges, competitiveness, or stability?
- And the list goes on…

Gathering answers during the OC assessment can be done in numerous ways, you just need to find the best method that suits your needs, timing and budget. These may include:

Individual Meetings

Individual interviews are a source of rich information because they provide detail and perspective. This format is effective as long as participants are confident that their individual responses will be kept confidential. Be sure to include employees from all departments, functions and levels of the organization, including top leaders.

Your success in this effort is directly related to collecting accurate information, understanding expectations and gaining buy-in from the top. Start with top leaders since their schedules may pose significant challenges. Where possible include interviews with former top leaders who have moved on.

Focus Group Meetings

Face-to-face focus group meetings can help expedite the process and save time while still providing rich information. To protect the validity of the information received, only invite participants that are confident enough to openly share opinions and information in a group setting. Ask open-ended questions to generate discussion and help encourage open, honest feedback. Limit your focus group to around 6-8 participants.

Anonymous Closed-Ended Surveys

Once you have collected feedback from a sampling of the overall population, you can then consolidate and analyze that information to develop a closed-ended survey to be completed by all employees. Consider using at least one open-ended question to encourage specific comments.

For example, when I worked for Black & Decker in the Power Tool Division, we had long assembly lines with 25-30 people on them and employees often had no idea what the end product was they were assembling. Without fully understanding the magnitude and importance of their contribution, employees can't become fully engaged in the success of the organization.

When employees (and customers) connect with the organization's purpose and reason for existence, they go beyond being an employee to being a business partner committed to the organization's success, secure in their belonging and seeing how they directly contribute.

It's important that employees work together for a shared purpose and outcome; something they can personally relate to in terms of why the organization exists and why their contribution makes a difference. That 'why' is not to have a job and get paid or to create profits – those are outcomes not purposes. Purpose is also not about "what" the organization does – the products or services it provides. Rather, purpose is about articulating <u>why</u> the work you do is important. This seemingly simple question provides significance for the organization and each employee.

What do your answers say about what your organization *really* values? This is NOT the time to gloss over anything. Glossing over issues is what got you to where you are today. This is the time for brutal honesty.

As you review the answers to these questions ask yourself "What does this say about our organization's actual values, as opposed to espoused values?"

Step 2: Identify what employees believe is the purpose of your organization. Why do they think it exists and how do they connect with that purpose? Are they engaged with your organization and believe they can make a meaningful contribution to its success? Do employees believe their work is important?

This step will help identify how employees view the organization and their connection to it. During this step you will want to explore questions such as:

1.   Why does the organization exist?
2.   What is the purpose of this organization?
3.   How/why is the work you do important?
4.   How does ABC organization make a difference to society as a whole through the product(s) or service(s) you provide?
5.   How do you make a contribution to society through the work you do?

6.   How would you describe your relationship to the organization's vision, mission, values, etc.?

7.   How would you describe this organization?

8.   How would you describe a person's connection to the organization?

Step 3: What Behavior Standards Do Your Philosophies Establish?

In Step 2, you discovered how employees view the purpose behind your organization and how they believe they can connect on both a rational and emotional level with who your organization is and what your organization does.

Now, take a look at how we expect employees to behave and make decisions based on those values. While Purpose is about "why" your organization exists, your Philosophies explain "how" the values are *intended* to be demonstrated or "lived" by every employee every day. This "how" is critical to a strong, differentiating OC.

Case in Point: In the early 2000s, I was hired to work with a company on the verge of losing the strong, differentiating culture they had spent 25+ years developing and reinforcing. A culture that had proved vital to both their business success (quality, safety, profitability, etc.) and their employee engagement success. The reason: they hired a new plant manager who had no idea what the culture was and didn't care. He came in with a "my way or the highway" attitude and within 6 months disengaged what was previously a highly engaged workforce.

Under his leadership employees were no longer asked to participate in team problem solving initiatives. The strong suggestion program, which was really an improvement implementation system was dismantled. Employee ideas were no longer valued and were even belittled. Employees who had previously been used as tour guides to provide firsthand accounts of quality, safety and process improvements when executives or customers toured the plant, were replaced by managers who took credit for those improvements. Under his leadership engaged employees committed to making a difference and invested in the success of the business were essentially hidden from view, reduced to only following the instructions given without question.

When I arrived and started analyzing the situation, it became clear the new plant manager had no idea how important culture was or the competitive advantage it provided. And worse yet, he didn't care. His reign continued for about three more months before he was fired because he didn't "fit" the culture. Within weeks of his departure, performance, employee engagement, attitude and commitment all improved. Employees stopped "checking their brains at the door" and once again got involved in the business and how to make it better. Leaders learned a valuable lesson – that you couldn't just hire the candidate with the best credentials. You had to hire someone who valued the culture and understood its significance.

In successful organizations, employees at all levels consciously and consistently use the organization's philosophies to guide their decisions and actions.

Values usually remain constant, but philosophies or how we expect employees to demonstrate those values can change, especially when new leaders or employees of influence are brought on board. If these changes aren't monitored and made with conscious intention even a great culture can erode and eventually be lost altogether. Consider when an organization experiences a merger or acquisition or when a new department manager or CEO is hired. They may or may not share the organization's values, and they may have a different interpretation of how employees are expected to behave.

How are Employees Expected to Demonstrate the Values?

Evaluate the consistency of what is expected of employees in how they "live" the values when making everyday decisions and taking action by asking employees the following:

1. Based on the values you cited earlier, what instructions and training are provided to employees on how to demonstrate those values in daily interactions and when things get tough?
2. Do employees follow these guidelines?
3. If not, when don't they follow them?
4. Are there any consequences if they aren't followed?
5. If specific guidelines don't exist, how do employees know what's expected? How will they know how to behave and make decisions?
6. Are some levels of the organization expected to uphold the values but others aren't? Can some employees decide on the fly when to uphold the values and when to make exceptions? Are some employees not expected to uphold the values at all?
7. Do the philosophy statements change based on the severity of a crisis?
8. Do they change based on whose involved in a particular situation or event?
9. When seeming exceptions to the values are made, do leaders and/or others take time to explain why they made the decision(s) they did and how it upholds the values or why it was necessary to deviate from the normal expectations?
10. Are there any philosophies that everyone must live by for the organization to compete and thrive?

Allow employees to provide information unimpeded and confidentially – even if they are missing vital information. Remember this is their perception of your OC and perception is reality!

Remember, to preserve and reinforce your organization's philosophies. Great care must be taken to develop and implement philosophy statements and training programs to clearly communicate how your organization defines its stated values. Your philosophies should also include examples of the types of decisions expected to be made in various situations to uphold and "live" the values in everyday interactions.

When dealing with philosophies, it's important to understand and appreciate the organization's history and founding and why things are done the way they are done. But be careful not to become mindlessly entrenched in the old ways of doing things just because "that's the way we've always done it". Otherwise you risk losing your objectivity and innovation. Instead, when considering doing things differently or making decisions in a different way, examine your values and philosophies and compare the new ways being considered to ensure your actions support and reinforce them. Otherwise, your actions will be contrary to your espoused values and philosophies, fragmenting your culture and dividing your team.

For example: One of Eaton Corporation's espoused values is to:

• Be honest, fair and open.

Their supporting philosophy statement articulates that "… Our communications with one another are open, honest and timely. Eaton provides the regular, timely information necessary to enable employees to do their jobs effectively, to make decisions and to achieve the company's goals; employees respond by giving the company their ideas and feedback. The result is an ongoing candid dialogue about the business that is fundamental to continuous improvement."

When leaders are developing meeting agendas both the value (to be open, honest and fair) and the philosophy (to communicate in a timely manner, provide information needed by employees to do their jobs and to solicit and expect feedback and ideas from employees in a two-way dialogue) are considered to ensure the content, format and detail meet these criteria. In other words, do their actions support both the stated value and how they are expected to behave? If either of these elements are missing or are contrary, leaders are expected to reconsider and revise their approach.

Step 4: Actions Speak Louder than Words

During Steps 1-3, you've been assessing employees' *perceptions* of you organization's purpose, values and philosophies. During step four, you're attempting to discover why your employees perceive your OC the way they do and how that supports or refutes your desired OC. During Step 4, you're asking employees to provide specific examples of actions, decisions, or behaviors that have led to their perceptions.

Case in Point: Recently the National Football League (NFL) has been in the news regarding their response to the actions of some of their players who have been charged with domestic violence, child abuse, assault and even murder. Take two examples: Ray Rice of the Baltimore Ravens and Adrian Peterson of the Minnesota Vikings. Ray Rice was suspended following the release of a video showing him punching his then-fiancée in the face during an argument. After knocking her unconscious in the hotel elevator, he dragged her body out into the hallway. Within a week of Rice's suspension, Adrian Peterson was charged with child abuse after beating his stepson with a "switch", or what my parents would have commonly referred to as a "hickory", so badly that he actually injured the boy. Clearly the NFL's official policy on domestic violence was perceived differently by some of the players as demonstrated by their actions.

What Does The OC Equation™ Reveal About the OC of the NFL?

Using **The OC Equation™**, based on the NFL's actions, let's consider fan perception of the NFL's OC:

The NFL's website says it values:

- Performance & Teamwork
- Tradition & Innovation

- Diversity
- Learning

They define their Philosophies as:

- **Integrity** - We safeguard the integrity of the game. We are ethical in all of our dealings with fans, clubs, business partners, and each other. We follow through on our words with action. We are honest and direct. We create an environment that inspires trust and confidence.
- **Performance & Teamwork** - We expect from everyone in our organization the highest level of performance and commitment to our mission and values. We set the highest standards and challenge ourselves to keep improving. We are accountable for our results and consistently measure our progress. We make smart and informed business decisions. We work together, sharing knowledge, information and other resources to attain the best results. We focus on organizational objectives, not individual agendas.
- **Tradition & Innovation** - We recognize that the NFL's traditions are an asset, but we also embrace change. We do not rest on our accomplishments. We seek new ways of performing in response to fan interests, technology, and the best practices and business models of other organizations. We balance the need to change with the utmost respect for what has been accomplished. We are thoughtful and deliberate in our thinking, and always consider the long-term consequences of our decisions.
- **Diversity** - We create an organization that represents, supports and celebrates diversity, while also embracing our shared interests. We represent and respect a wide range of human differences, personal experiences and cultural backgrounds for the benefit of the organization and our employees as individuals.

We provide each employee with an opportunity to achieve his or her full potential.

- **Learning** - We take individual responsibility for learning, personal growth, and career development. We actively support, as an organization, opportunities for individual development, but we recognize that personal talent and initiative will primarily drive individual growth. We encourage employees to seek learning opportunities both inside and outside the workplace.

Now that we know the NFL's Values & Philosophies, it's time to evaluate those against their actions. This is where the rubber actually hits the road. Forget the niceties that are written and displayed for the outside world, what do they *really* value as evidenced through their *ACTIONS*? Or to put it another way, how should a fan perceive the NFL's OC?

You "Live" Your OC through Your ACTIONS

When evaluating the NFL's culture, we begin by looking at their actions. In other words, what does the NFL hire for, reward and fire for? Since January 2000, there have been a total of 731 arrests and alleged criminal incidents involving NFL players, including at least three players arrested for involvement in the deaths of other people; Aaron Hernandez, Jovan Belcher and Josh Bent.

So, based on the ACTIONS of the NFL, it appears their OC is one of "win at any costs and protect high performing players no matter what" (unless of course they murder at least 3 people or commit suicide). Short of that, players get a slap on the wrist for inappropriate behavior. So, it would appear that the stated value of Integrity is not "lived" in the NFL culture.

According to a recent Wall Street Journal article, "In 1925, when Harold "Red" Grange—the Galloping Ghost, who lighted up the backfield at the University of Illinois—signed a pro contract with the

Chicago Bears, his college coach Robert Zuppke disavowed the star halfback, declaring him persona non grata. As Columbia coach Lou Little said, "I'm out to make men first, and then football players." What kind of a man would waste his life in that goon squad of a league?"

Apparently, based on the elements of **The OC Equation™** and the actual actions of the NFL, the commissioner and the owners, gone are the days when **integrity** meant "making men first and then football players". The NFL has allowed their accidental culture to take over resulting in a no holds barred mentality. Following the recent bad publicity and grass roots efforts of many fans and activists, today the NFL is hypersensitive to employee behavior, not because of their values and philosophies, but because of the potential monetary hit to their brand.

And that's how it is with OC – it's not what you say, it's what you do that really determines your OC and if it can be used as a competitive advantage.

Your values and philosophies are meaningless unless employees' actions are representative of them. The NFL clearly demonstrates this, doesn't it? When actions match your organization's values and principles it creates stability and confidence and provides the foundation for an OC as a sustainable competitive advantage in the marketplace.

Moving Forward

Now that you've completed the OC Assessment, take time to review the results. It's important to keep an open mind and avoid becoming defensive. The OC Assessment isn't a criticism; it's a tool to help your organization improve and gain a competitive advantage. With that thought in mind, review the results considering the following points:

- What cultural strengths have been highlighted through the OC Assessment regarding your current culture?
- What factors are hindering achievement of the business strategy or are misaligned with one another?

- What factors are detrimental to the health and productivity of your workplace?
- What values, philosophies and factors need to be further encouraged and reinforced?
- Which factors need to change to match the desired OC?
- What new beliefs and behaviors need to be promoted?
- What did you learn about your 'real' culture based on employee feedback?
- What cultural strengths have been highlighted by your OC Assessment of the current culture?
- What factors are hindering your strategy or are misaligned with one another?
- What factors are detrimental to the health and productivity of the workplace?
- What factors need to be encouraged and reinforced?
- Which factors need to change?
- What new beliefs and behaviors need to be promoted and reinforced through expenditure of resources?

You've come a long way. You've defined your current OC. It's time to move to the next step which is defining the OC you desire. To get to the OC desired, you'll need to create a plan for changing and improving the areas of the organization that are not aligned with your desired culture. The goal here is to develop a plan that will close gaps between where you are now and where you want to be. That's what we'll explore in the next chapter.

The OC Equation™ in Action
1   Conduct an OC Assessment to identify your 'current state'.
2   Don't just assume you know what your OC is.
3   Get others involved in the assessment.
4   Be prepared to be shocked. .
5   Remember, ACTIONS speak louder than words.

Chapter 8

Moving the Needle to Get to Your Ultimate OC

"No pain, no gain!"
"An organization's ability to learn, and translate
that learning into action rapidly, is the
ultimate competitive advantage."
~ Jack Welch, Retired CEO – General Electric

Setting the Ball in Motion -
Gathering and Analyzing Marketing Materials

With the OC Assessment complete, it's time to embark on phase II – auditing how well your *Actions* are aligned with your espoused values and philosophies as opposed to what you actually value and reinforce.

Begin by reviewing every piece of internal and external marketing collateral that exists in and for your organization, including materials published and distributed to employees and other stakeholders that explain what you have to offer, what your organization is about, what you expect of others and what they can expect from you. Materials include electronic or printed e-brochures, newsletters, fact sheets, press releases, employee handbooks, internal memos, external letters, and annual reports.

As you review the marketing materials, ask yourself, "What do we say is the reason our organization exists?" "What values and philosophies do we say are important?" "What commitments do we make?"

"What do we say is important to our organization?" Don't just look for the obvious – you may not have a defined "core values" statement, you may have to read between the lines. What would an objective third party say, based on what you published is important? How would they describe the values your organization is based on? Compile a list and then review it for common themes and any inconsistencies.

Comparing Employee Feedback

After completing the marketing materials review, compare that to the feedback gathered in the OC assessment. Do employees and leaders agree? In other words, do employees articulate the same values and philosophies your marketing materials portray as important? Do your actions support those values and philosophies?

Don't just look at the words used to describe your values and philosophies – examine your actions! For example, do you say team work is valued, but have reward and incentive systems that focus on the results of individual achievers? Does your marketing material indicate a core value of integrity, but you reward taking shortcuts to get product out the door as long as the customer doesn't notice or complain?

The feedback received from the OC Assessment may be hard to take. It may even seem that some employees have an axe to grind – and that may be true for some. But remember to keep your eye on the prize – your goal is to objectively assess your current OC, compare that to your desired OC and create definitive action plans to close those gaps and create the culture needed for a sustainable competitive advantage.

Without facing harsh realities, you won't identify problem areas so action plans can be implemented to effect the changes necessary to enhance your OC and create a sustainable competitive advantage for your organization. If you gloss over information, become defensive or ignore it altogether, you'll never be able to get to the culture you want and need to thrive and compete.

Defining What You Believe the Purpose Is

How would you answer the same questions that you asked employees?

1. Why does the organization exist?
2. What is the purpose of this organization?
3. How/why is the work you do important?
4. How does ABC organization make a difference to society as a whole through the product(s) or service(s) you provide?
5. How do you make a contribution to society through the work you do?
6. How would you describe your relationship to the organization's vision, mission, values, etc.?
7. How would you describe this organization?
8. How would you describe people's connection to the organization?

Do your responses and expectations align with the information gleaned from the focus groups, interviews and surveys? Is there consensus? What themes, if any, emerge? Is there a common driving purpose that compels employees to get out of bed in the morning, come to work and make a difference? Or, is it every man (and woman) for themselves?

Critical data arises where differences between the two lists are noted. Analyze the reasons behind the differences. Is it because silos exist? Are there turf battles going on? Do other leaders subscribe to other values and philosophies that drive their actions? Is there a lack of communication across and within departments? For example, if employees, department managers, supervisors, executive leaders, customers, and vendors believe there is a different purpose, it's likely that functional or department silos exist where employees are working toward their defined purpose (read: Agenda) with little collaboration, information sharing, resource sharing, or consideration for the overall good of the organization. Not only does this segment your human resources, it also takes a toll on your budget, discouraging team work and encouraging duplication of efforts and waste.

Aligning Philosophies

Take a deep breath. You've done the heavy lifting by comparing what the organization says it values with what employees believe is valued. Now we'll work to align your philosophies with your espoused values so they are consistently reflected in employee's actions.

Values are meaningless unless they are backed up with well-defined philosophy statements outlining how the values are intended to be demonstrated when making both minor and major decisions and through employee behavior.

Begin by reviewing the responses employees provided during the OC Assessment. What do employees say is expected of them and how they behave in various situations? Do they outline actions and behaviors that are consistent with what you expect? Are they consistent with what you've published in any marketing collateral?

Case in Point: It is quite possible that when Kenneth Lay founded Enron in 1985 he really believed in the values of Integrity, Communication, Respect, and Excellence. However, after Jeffrey Skilling was hired the values changed. Enron executives used accounting loopholes, special purpose entities, and poor financial reporting to hide millions of dollars in debt from investors and regulators and pressured Arthur Andersen, their external accounting firm, to ignore the issues. Clearly, Enron executives were following a different set of values and philosophies than those originally held by the founder. Are lower level leaders in your organization or influential informal leaders setting different expectations for how employees behave? Have sub-cultures emerged in your organization with different values and philosophies?

If your organization is like so many and believes that the values and philosophies are intuitive and employees "know" what's expected in terms of how they make decisions and how they conduct themselves in interactions with others, it's time to develop and implement actual philosophy statements and conduct training to get employees on board.

Warning: Don't be surprised if you lose some employees (at all levels) once you begin making these changes and enforcing the values and philosophies. Some employees like having little structure and guidance and will be very uncomfortable with the new expectations. In addition, remember, these changes will upset the natural flow of work in your organization and will make employees uncomfortable because how they achieved results in the past may not work in this new environment. Your employees will struggle for a while with changing bad habits that worked for them and replacing those bad habits with good habits that support the positive OC needed to be competitive. Not only will you have to implement a new OC, you'll also have to provide employees, including leaders, with the tools needed to effectively make the changes.

Beware of Managing to the
Lowest Common Denominator (LCD)

Managing based on the idea of the lowest common denominator (LCD) is based on a negative view of people and overall human nature and is intended to provide protections from the weakest link in the proverbial chain.

The Rule of Expectations - You get what you expect. We've all heard a variation of this. People will live up to your expectations. If you set your expectations low, people will live down to them. If you set them high, people will live up to them, so you may as well set them high. This is known as the Rule of Expectations. Like it or not, people (and employees) tend to make decisions based on how others expect them to behave or perform and fulfill expectations – whether positive or negative.

Expectations have a powerful impact on those who respect and trust us, but they also can have a huge impact on those we barely know – because human nature attempts to gain respect, seeks approval and desires to be liked. In business, you've likely heard the adage, "What gets measured, gets done". Well, the same is true for your values and philosophies and how you expect those to be "lived" every day. What is expected is what actually happens. Your expectations can become self-fulfilling prophecies and can actually lead to people improvements or people destruction. If you express your expectations in terms of doubts, skepticism and lack of confidence, you will likely get those results. On the other hand, if you show confidence in people and expect them to succeed, you will likely see that result.

John Maxwell and Jim Dornan in their book, *Becoming a Person of Influence*, put it this way, "Those who believe in our ability do more than stimulate us. They create for us an atmosphere in which it becomes easier to succeed".

The Rule of Expectation in Action

Several years ago, my son, Matthew, was struggling to find his direction and purpose in life. He had been through a bad break up with his girlfriend, another close friend was brutally murdered by her stepbrother and his dad, and I moved from Ohio to Tennessee leaving him alone in Ohio at Bowling Green State University. Needless to say he felt his world was spinning out of control and his outlook and grades showed it.

It wasn't long after that he decided a new direction was needed so he moved to South Carolina to attend school and be closer to family. This decision wasn't the answer to his quest either and he continued to struggle to discover what his life path should be. He continued to flounder for a couple of years. Starting and stopping school, even moving to Texas with his older adopted brother to work for a while before going back to school yet again. But nothing worked! Nothing motivated him, and worse yet, he developed a mental image where he expected to fail. After struggling for a couple more quarters, he decided he would try real estate working for his grandmother. He jumped into it with gusto thinking it was a quick fix to his lack of direction and focus. He worked diligently throughout the course and then took the national real estate exam. He passed with flying colors, but he still had to pass the state exam to become licensed in South Carolina.

The state exam wasn't as easy and he failed it – his score on the exam was close but not close enough to pass. Not discouraged, he signed up to take it again. He dove back into the books and studied like crazy. Again, he failed a second time – this time by one question!

Disappointed and convinced he would never succeed, he called me for advice. He was sure he was a complete failure and would never make anything out of his life – in other words, all his expectations were being met!

When he asked me what he would do if he failed it again, led by the grace of God, I told him he would keep trying. Then I said the magic words; "I know you can do it!" I told him it was just a test and it was no reflection of him as a person if he didn't pass it. He would just have to get up and try again. But then I reiterated, "I know you can do it!" Those were the magic words. I could literally hear the relief in his voice. My expectation was clear – I knew he could do it – whether it took one additional attempt or ten. So now he was trying to live up to my high expectations instead of his low expectations.

The next day he went to the testing center with an expectation that he could, in fact, pass this exam – and he did, with flying colors! That simple expectation changed not only that outcome, it carried over into every other aspect of his life! Now that he had become a licensed real estate agent his confidence knew no bounds. He began setting other goals and expectations and his grades and work quality soared!

That was 3 years ago and today, he's obtained his Associate's Degree in Business, he's a successful real estate agent with Prudential Real Estate and is finishing his bachelor's degree at Southern Wesleyan University. The Rule of Expectation in action!

Managing to the Lowest Common Denominator (LCD)

To help ensure employees behave in ways consistent with your values, it's important to clearly communicate *HOW* you expect employees to act. This is best done through well-defined philosophies. **The OC Equation™** defines philosophies as the embodiment of its values. In other words it's how the values are *intended* to be demonstrated or "lived" through every day interactions and decisions. As you align philosophies and values be aware of the rule of expectations, discussed above and the LCD which we'll look at now.

In business it's often easier to manage to the lowest common denominator (LCD) because there is a perception that if we account for every possible fallacy, we won't have to actually think. Leading in an LCD environment is often expressed in such terms as: employees are dumb, they can't be trusted to do things right (or do the right thing), they always screw up, they will steal you blind, they're lazy and so on.

In all organizations errors will happen, misunderstandings will occur, some things that should happen won't, and some things that shouldn't happen will. But that shouldn't discourage you as a leader from striving for excellence and setting high expectations, including that employees live up to the organization's values and philosophies and support the OC.

In an LCD culture, managers believe that the errors, mistakes, and indifference of a few are the rule, not the exception. And based on the Rule of Expectation – they are probably right! As a result, managers attempt to control every aspect of the work environment. This response inevitably leads to micro-management tactics that instill fear and threat into the organization further eroding trust, performance and results. When threat is imposed, employees mentally check out, they stop caring about quality, safety, performance and responsibility. After all, that's all that's expected of them.

Employees need leaders to help them focus their energy. With focused energy, employees understand the organization's purpose, vision, mission, goals and objectives and how they can contribute to success. Henry Cloud, the author of "Boundaries" calls it the Boundaries of Attention, what employees should focus their attention on for success.

The Science of a Positive OC

The brain functions in an emotional climate and high performance only happens in a positive emotional climate. For the brain to operate at an optimal level three things must be available: glucose, oxygen and relationship. These things fuel the brain and allow employees to perform at maximum level. The first two deal with providing employees with a healthful environment – for example, clear, safe air to breathe and breaks where employees can refuel on healthy food. But for optimum performance employees also need healthy, positive relationships.

When a positive emotional climate is established, the neurotransmitters in the brain that are needed to complete complex functions (problem solving, adaptation, examining alternative solutions, being creative, persevering, etc.) release positive chemicals needed to fuel performance. Conversely, in a negative environment, those same neurotransmitters release different chemicals needed by the body to react to a threat. The natural fight or flight reaction when faced with danger is fueled by different chemicals released into the body. In OCs where leaders create a toxic environment that threaten employee's spirits, the brain stops thinking so it can simply react. When this happens employees will either resist (fight), sent out their resumes (flight) or become paralyzed and acquiesce. Employees who experience fear and intimidation shut down and cease to think dooming the organization to failure.

Positive OCs fuel performance. But don't mistake a positive OC with unrealistic unicorns and rainbows. In organizations with positive OCs, employees are still faced with challenges, negative experiences, and fear, but it's a good fear, not threatening fear. Good fear means transparent communications, even about business conditions that are negative, but in a respectful manner of empowerment that allows employees to continue thinking so they can cope and adapt to the situation and make good decisions to get appropriate results.

It's Worse Than the Pareto Principle

The Pareto Principle says that 80% of the effects come from 20% of the causes. If this is true, 80% of the problems in any organization are caused by 20% of the employees. In a LCD environment, managers don't focus on how to effectively and efficiently serve the 95-98% of employees who do things right. Instead they dedicate the majority of their time, resources and energy to anticipating and resolving the problems caused by only 2-5% of the employees. The fact that exceptions are never eliminated further reinforces the need for managers to accommodate the LCD. And the vicious cycle persists – management's inability to prevent exceptions drives more focus on increasing resources to resolve the potential, future problems of a tiny minority at the expense of trusting the vast majority.

Management by LCD is inefficient in delivering services and costly in fiscal terms. It takes a human toll, demoralizing employees with low expectations which lowers performance across the board. It prevents leaders from capitalizing on the strengths, knowledge and initiative of team members which further contributes to the ineffectiveness of the organization and the vicious reinforcement of the LCD cycle.

The Courage to Lead

To avoid management by LCD, take a step back and question your assumptions. "Have expectations been established for upholding the OC?" "Do our philosophies define what the values are and how you expect employees to act in support of the OC?" "Do you reward behavior that upholds your stated values or something else?" "Do you concentrate a lot of your efforts on what people might do wrong or do you expect the majority to do what's right?"; "Do you write your policies and procedures for the 2% that will abuse them or the 98%

who won't?"; "Do you try to compensate for possible failures or do you expect success?"; "Do you think employees are dumb or do you think they are the key to your success? Do you establish and communicate the right expectations?" "Do you plan for failure or do you plan for success?" If your responses to these questions indicate LCD thinking, it's time to try something different.

Getting new employees started off on the right foot is critical to setting both behavior and performance expectations and assimilating them quickly into your OC. Consider the following new hire welcome letter:

> Dear [Employee Name],
>
> Welcome to the team! I am pleased to have you working with us. You were selected for employment based on the attributes you possess that appear to match the qualities I look for in an employee.
>
> I'm looking forward to seeing you grow and develop into an outstanding employee that exhibits our values and philosophies, demonstrates a high level of care, concern, and compassion for others and is committed to high performance. As we all work together to align around our organization's purpose to achieve our collective vision and mission, I am sure you will find your work to be rewarding, challenging, and meaningful.
>
> As a member of our team I expect your best each day. Know that I am concerned about your development and that my door is always open. The keys to your success will be being dependable, reliable, showing openness, follow-through, attentiveness, leadership, followership, documentation, and following our policies and guidelines. By engaging in these things, you will be successful and so will [Company Name]. Your professional growth is of utmost concern for me personally, because if you are growing our clients will grow as well.

Please take your time and review our values, philosophies and goals so you can know what is expected and how to make a positive contribution. Again, I look forward to seeing you grow as a professional while enhancing the lives of the clients entrusted in our care.

Sincerely,

[Manager Name]

Human nature is such that most people want to please others by living up to their expectations. By setting high expectations early and providing coaching and counseling, you take a giant step toward positive performance and behavior, rather than managing to the LCD. I know it seems impossible, but there are tremendous advantages including operational efficiencies, fiscal savings and human successes to dumping an "LCD" management style. It won't be easy, but the payoffs are tremendous – after all – no pain, no gain – right?

So, challenge yourself and those you influence in your organization by asking some provocative questions: "Do we have the courage to lead a team based on values and philosophies? Are we willing to support actions that uphold our values and philosophies instead of the LCD?" If your answer is yes, review your policies, procedures, rules and decisions and decide what needs to change to shift your focus from low or inconsistent expectations to high expectations – and then watch the Rule of Expectations take over.

But remember, you didn't get here overnight and you won't change overnight. It takes, time, diligence, patience, reinforcement and intentional leadership. It won't be easy and you and your team will make mistakes, but if you expect everyone to learn from those mistakes and rise to the occasion, they will and your results will soar.

Thriving Through Meaningful Actions

So far, on this journey you've completed the OC Assessment in Chapter 7 and compared the employees' responses to leaders' responses and the organization's marketing materials to identify gaps between your current OC and your desired OC. You've also taken steps to align values and philosophies and avoid the Rule of Expectations and LCD. Now I want to provide you with an example of an organization who has mastered the competitive advantage of OC as a business strategy. Let's take a look at how Netflix has aligned their values and philosophies and intertwined them into the very fabric of their organization so they are reflected in employees' actions.

Case In Point: Netflix says its culture is based on the "*behaviors* and *skills* that we particularly *value* in fellow employees". It has established nine (9) behaviors and skills that are particularly valued (what gets people hired, fired or rewarded):

1. Judgment – employees' ability to make wise decisions (people, technical, business, and creative) despite ambiguity.
2. Communication – employees' ability to listen well, instead of reacting fast, so they can better understand.
3. Impact – employees accomplish amazing amounts of important work.
4. Curiosity – employees learn rapidly and eagerly.
5. Innovation – employees re-conceptualize issues to discover practical solutions to hard problems.
6. Courage – employees say what they think even if it is controversial.
7. Passion - employees inspire others with their thirst for excellence.
8. Honesty – employees are known for candor and directness.
9. Selflessness – employees seek what is best for Netflix, rather than best for themselves or the group.

As you can see, Netflix not only states their values, they also provide definitions of those values in the form of philosophies that indicate how those values are expected to be implemented in everyday interactions with co-workers, direct reports, vendors, suppliers and other stakeholders. Then they go a step further and provide employees with specific values-based training. In that training they note that employees should, "question actions inconsistent with our values - Part of the Courage value, akin to the honor code pledge: 'I will not lie, nor cheat, nor steal, *nor tolerate those who do'*. All of us are responsible for value consistency".

Setting Priorities

Establishing and protecting your OC isn't just the job of executives and leaders, it's everyone's job. But **The OC Equation™** must be fulfilled so your actions consistently uphold your values as stated in your philosophies.

As with any change, it's important to set priorities to avoid overwhelming yourself and your organization. As the old saying goes, you eat an elephant one bite at a time. So begin by identifying where your intended culture is different from your actual culture and set specific priorities for making changes to move the organization in the right direction. This is going to take a considerable amount of focused effort. You're going to have to sell your ideas, values and philosophies to all employees and that may be difficult. People don't mind change, but they do mind being changed.

The Power of Compounding Culture

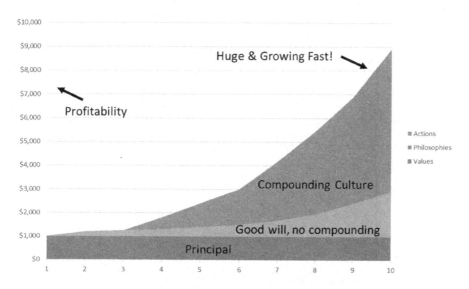

The Power of Compounding Culture occurs when you make an emotional investment in your organization and employees where the initial investment begins to feed on itself to either strengthen or degrade your organization. **The OC Equation™** is comprised of values, philosophies and actions that create the outcome and momentum upon which compounding culture multiplies.

Let me explain. Values create the foundation (guiding principles) of how your organization is expected to run and every decision that's made. Philosophies and your philosophy statements articulate how the values are expected to come to life and be consistently demonstrated and reinforced throughout the organization. Actions are what creates the momentum to propel the OC forward.

If actions contradict those statements, stakeholders (including your employees) will disregard your words, believing rather in your actions and it's those actions that will ultimately dictate your OC (good or bad). When all three are aligned and working in tandem both employee and business needs are met and your organization begins experiencing the power of compounding culture. When these elements begin feeding off each other, the results are nothing short of extraordinary.

Practical Example

Let's take two very different companies with leaders who ascribe to very different values, philosophies and leadership styles, which are evident in their actions.

Autocratic Eddie – He believes that he is in charge and is responsible for making all the decisions of the department. He believes employees can't be trusted to make decisions because if you give employees an inch they will take a mile. He also believes employees come to work late, leave early and steal from the company. Eddie believes very strict, detailed policies and procedures are required so employees know the rules and can be disciplined for violations.

Because of Autocratic Eddie's perspective, when new employees start work, he immediately tells them they are on a 90-day probationary period and their ability, attitude, and attendance will be measured before a final decision is made on their future employment status. In addition, he requires his employees to punch a time clock and when absences occur they're docked pay and each absence is carefully tracked and monitored. Autocratic Eddie's employees are required to work the day before and after holidays so they don't arbitrarily become "sick" to extend a holiday weekend.

Trusting Terry – She believes that the best decisions come from involving employees at all levels, especially those directly impacted by the decisions. She believes most employees are trustworthy and hardworking and they care as much about the company as she does. As a result, she believes general guidelines are all that's needed to manage because 98% of employees act as adults and can be trusted and treated with respect and dignity.

Trusting Terry considers new employees to be full-fledged team members from day one and expects them to immediately contribute to the success of the organization. Her employees don't punch a time clock, rather they self-record their time on time sheets that are turned in at the end of each week. Terry establishes the expectation that employees report all absences on their time sheets and trusts them to do so to ensure the company has accurate payroll records. Employees with habitual absences are coached individually for improvement and she never mentions to her employees that they need to work the day before and after a holiday, but come to think of it, she's never had a reason to.

As you read these two examples, you may begin to see the power of compounding culture. In Autocratic Eddie's environment, it is likely that with each passing day, he gets less and less from his employees as they become unmotivated clock watchers who do just enough to get by because that's all that's expected. This negative culture compounds and begins to erode the engagement, morale, motivation and ultimately the profitability of both current and future employees. Good employees leave the organization to find a strong positive culture where their needs are met and they are trusted and appreciated while talented candidates avoid interviewing or decline offers because no one wants to work in a toxic environment.

Trusting Terry has a very different experience. She develops relationships with her employees. She demonstrates genuine concern for them as individuals and as a team. She engages employees in decisions that affect them and seeks their input. In other words, she trusts her employees and treats them with respect and dignity and they do the same in return. The idea of giving a little bit more is mutual and based on trust and respect. Rather than writing policies for the 2% that will abuse them, policies are written for the 98% who do it right. In Terry's organization, performance and profits soar. Current employees are engaged and invested in this work environment and rarely leave and which attracts more good employees continuing the compounding effect.

In short, it doesn't matter what you wish your culture was or what culture you "think" you have, what really matters is what culture you "actually" have based on who's hired, fired and rewarded.

In this chapter we completed a review of the current OC by comparing marketing materials with what employees said about the organization's values. Based on that review, we looked at how to align values and philosophies by acknowledging the Rule of Expectation and avoiding LCD. Finally, we looked at setting priorities as you move forward with changing the OC. It's all part of the journey toward The OC Equation™.

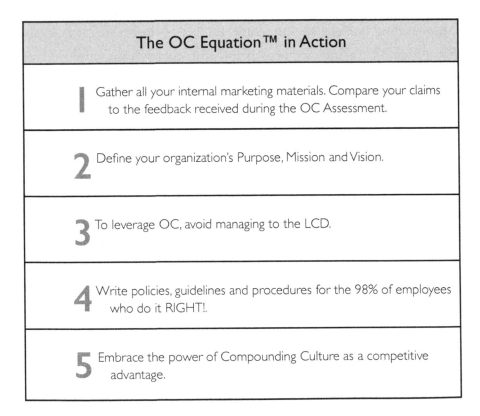

The OC Equation™ in Action
1 Gather all your internal marketing materials. Compare your claims to the feedback received during the OC Assessment.
2 Define your organization's Purpose, Mission and Vision.
3 To leverage OC, avoid managing to the LCD.
4 Write policies, guidelines and procedures for the 98% of employees who do it RIGHT!.
5 Embrace the power of Compounding Culture as a competitive advantage.

Part 3
Let's Go There!

Chapter 9

Making it Happen

"If you get the Culture right, most of the other stuff will just take care of itself" ~Tony Hseih, CEO, ZAPPOs

Up to this point in our journey, we've been concerned with definitions and the foundation of your OC. We've worked through defining what organizational culture (OC) is, your organization's purpose, vision and mission, and even your personal and organizational core values. Through the OC Assessment we even defined the current state of your OC. This final section is where we begin to build the OC your organization needs and wants to create a sustainable competitive advantage in every aspect of your business.

Keeping it Real

Organizational Cultures (OC) come in all shapes and sizes and there is no right or wrong culture for any particular organization. Each organization's culture works because it upholds their values and philosophies through their actions. You'd be surprised how many organizations try to emulate a successful company's OC. But you can't fake a culture. To be inspiring and create the competitive advantage you're looking for, your OC must be genuine.

Look at Netflix's culture again. Their training includes reinforcement that a "…great workplace is stunning colleagues. A great workplace is *not* day-care, espresso, health benefits, sushi lunches, nice offices, or big compensation, and we only do those [things] that are efficient at attracting stunning colleagues".

An OC that provides your organization with a competitive advantage has:

- Uncompromising values and philosophies.
- A compelling vision and purpose.
- Inspiring, visionary leaders.
- Stimulating surroundings.
- A "fits like a glove, I want to be there" brand.
- Strong communications.
- Embraced the power of conflict.
- Team dynamics.
- Empowered decision-making.
- Consistency.

Aligning Internal Actions

Now it's time to evaluate your internal actions and the extent to which they reinforce your organizational values and philosophies to create the desired OC. Here we will examine the internal processes and systems that dictate how leaders lead people and manage work flow and how employees work with each other. You'll assess the effectiveness of the organizational structure, work design, systems (including control systems) and processes for doing work, power structures, technology, internal rituals and routines, HR systems, such as attracting and retaining top talent, employee education and development, performance management, internal communications, reward and recognition and compensation.

To do this, we encourage you to conduct periodic OC audits to evaluate the alignment between your desired OC and the actions your systems and processes dictate. These audits are different from the earlier OC assessment in that the OC assessment was designed to evaluate your current OC. The audit is a review of the effectiveness of specific aspects of your business. When conducting the OC audit, you will be specifically measuring the degree to which each internal action, policy, guideline, procedure, process, etc. aligns with the desired OC.

Conducting an internal OC audit will help you evaluate each aspect of the internal workings of your organization. It includes an audit of your organizational structure, work design and systems (including control systems), and processes for doing work and interacting with others, power structures, technology, internal rituals and routines. It encompasses not only your HR practices, like recruiting, selection, onboarding, employee development, performance management, communications, rewards and recognition and compensation, but your business practices as well. During the OC audit, you will evaluate each internal action against the values and philosophies that are the cornerstone of your desired OC to ensure they support and reflect each attribute.

After completing an internal OC audit, the next step is to conduct an external OC audit to evaluate the degree of alignment that exists between your external actions and your desired OC. If your internal actions do not reflect the values and philosophies you purport to be keys to success, your OC will be meaningless – not worth the paper it's written on.

Linking The OC Equation™ to your DNA

Now it's time to look at the details of your internal organization's structure, policies, procedures and processes in an effort to evaluate if the espoused values, philosophies and actions (**The OC Equation™**) are consistently applied so as to be embedded in the DNA of your organization.

Aligning Organizational Structure, Work Design, and Systems

As you attempt to align these elements, you will be reviewing the organizational structure, job titles, how work is organized, how and by whom decisions are made, and the systems and processes used to do the work. While we often think of organizational structure in terms of the organization chart and formal reporting relationships, you must also consider the unwritten lines of power and influence that indicate whose contributions are most valued and who wields the most influence.

Organizational structures can vary widely; some are relatively flat while others are more hierarchical. Some are fairly static with well-defined job descriptions and department or functional reporting relationships while others are more dynamic with matrixes or informal reporting structures.

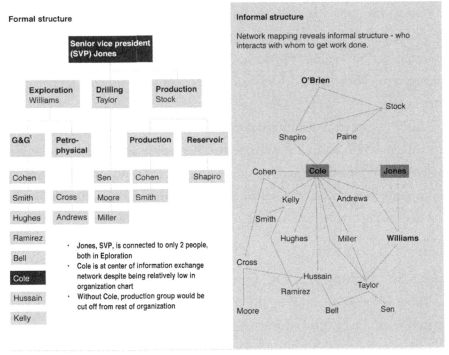

Formal structure

Informal structure

Network mapping reveals informal structure - who interacts with whom to get work done.

- Jones, SVP, is connected to only 2 people, both in Eploration
- Cole is at center of information exchange network despite being relatively low in organization chart
- Without Cole, production group would be cut off from rest of organization

¹Geological and geophysical.

Source: Robert L. Cross and Andrew Parker, *The Hidden Power of Social Networks*, Boston: HBS Press, 2004

Some are based on personal power to persuade and influence. There is no right or wrong organizational structure; it just needs to support the values and philosophies of your desired OC. Of course, even the most hierarchical organizations also have informal networks that are used to make things happen. If your organization is very formal and hierarchical the employees' emotional tie and loyalty will be closely linked (good

or bad) to their manager whereas in a less formal, networking organization, their loyalty is tied to their overall network.

As you look at how work is done and the systems which support that
work, evaluate how well those systems, and the actions that result, reinforce and support the values and philosophies of your OC. How things
get done affects employees on a daily basis. Make a note of the gaps so
an action plan can be devised to address any issues that impede your
desired OC. Questions to consider during this phase include:

- Is the structure flat or hierarchical? Formal or informal? Organic
  or mechanistic?
- Where are the formal lines of authority?
- Are there informal lines? If so, what are they and how do they
  work?
- Do employees get things done because they respect leaders or
  do they do things out of fear?
- Who has the real power in the organization?
- What do these people believe and champion within the
  organization?
- Who makes or influences decisions?
- How is this power used or abused?
- Which processes or procedures have the strongest controls?
  Weakest controls?
- As an organization are we generally loosely or tightly controlled?
- Do employees get rewarded for good work or penalized for poor
  work?
- How is good and poor work defined and by whom? Is it
  consistent?
- What reports are issued to keep control of operations, finance,
  etc...?

Aligning Talent Acquisition and Selection

Finding the right people for your organization is vital to preserving your OC. A Senior VP of mine once said, "Hiring is your organization's $1,000,000 decision, so make sure you do it well."

Review the results of the OC Assessment. What is your current hiring process? Does it align with your OC? What happens if a well-qualified candidate isn't a culture fit? Do they get hired anyway? No matter what you say your values and philosophies are it's your actions that make or break your desired culture as noted in **The OC Equation™**:

the OC equation™

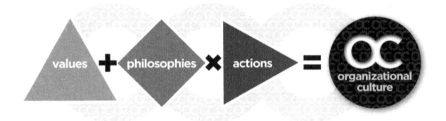

If you're truly committed to your OC, it starts with attracting and onboarding new employees. If it's not set up as an integral part of your talent acquisition process, you're going to be constantly reactive in maintaining your OC.

Protecting your culture starts with the talent you bring on board and the personal values and philosophies they bring with them. When new hires' values and philosophies don't match and integrate with the organization's values and philosophies, culture erosion can be the result. Companies committed to their OC understand the importance of hiring the right people. Netflix puts it this way, "…Diverse styles are fine – as long as [the] person embodies the 9 values."

How Zappos Protects Culture During the Hiring Process

At Zappos culture is so important that all new hires, regardless of position or level within the organization, are required to attend a four-week training period designed to immerse them in the company's strategy, culture, and obsession with customer service. To reinforce their commitment to the new hire, all new employees get paid their full salary during this onboarding experience.

A week or so into this immersive experience, Zappos does something virtually unheard of – they offer employees a bonus to quit! "The Offer" as it's called tells new hires, "If you quit today, we will pay you for the amount of time you've worked, plus we will offer you a month's salary in bonus." The offer is basically designed to bribe new employees to quit! You may be scratching your head and asking "why on earth would they do that?" In a word – culture. Zappos is so committed to protecting its culture it is willing to spend money to ensure it only keeps employees committed to it. If an employee is willing to take the company up on "The Offer", the employee obviously doesn't have the sense of commitment Zappos is looking for (about ten percent of new call-center employees take the money and run).

Recently, Amazon started offering a similar program. When informing stakeholders during the annual meeting about the program, CEO and Founder Jeff Bezos noted, "...*unhappy people make for unsuccessful companies. In the long run, an employee staying somewhere they don't want to be isn't healthy for the employee or the company. This is not, it should be stressed, an indictment of the organization or people who choose to leave. Great companies are great precisely because they stand for something special, different, distinctive. That means, almost by definition, that they are not for everybody. It takes a certain personality type to thrive in the extroverted, almost theatrical, culture of Zappos, or the driven, no-nonsense culture at Amazon. If there isn't the right fit, it makes perfect sense to quit.*"

In an organization committed to their OC, performance isn't just about business results; it's also about the people who produce those results. It doesn't matter if you lead teams at a Fortune 100 company or are hiring your first employees at a start-up. You need a hiring process that weeds out bad culture fits and produces candidates who will buy in and support your OC. To focus on both expertise and OC fit, we recommend you implement a dual focus interview process:

1. A skills interview that assesses the applicant's level of expertise regarding knowledge, skills, and abilities (KSAs), education and experience.

2. A culture interview to determine if they are a good fit for your OC. The culture interview should be designed specifically to help understand how well a candidate's personal values and philosophies align with your organizational values and philosophies. That commitment is what creates your competitive advantage.

After almost 30 years of working in various organizations and seeing a wide array of cultures, it's clear that 95-98% of all separations occur because of a lack of OC "fit", not a lack of KSAs. Focusing on OC is as important to your business success as a great business strategy.

When hiring for culture some basic questions might include: Describe for me your personal and professional values and philosophies, or tell me about a time you were part of a great team - what made it great? These are decent questions, but they only provide surface level insights into how well the candidate might fit into and support your organization. Try to develop more in-depth questions based on your organizational values and philosophies.

For example, if your OC focuses on providing exceptional customer service, you might ask questions such as:

- What does great customer service mean to you? In your last job, how did you know if your customer was satisfied?

- Give an example of a time you went above and beyond, why did you do it? Any regrets?
- What's the best work-related compliment you've ever received?

If your organization is all about innovation and change, you might ask questions such as:

- What new ideas have you recommended to your manager recently?
- How did you present those ideas? Were they adopted?
- Did you ever have an unpopular or minority view point and if so, did you stand up for it? What happened?
- How did you get into your current line of work? What did you want to be when you were growing up?
- Tell me about a time you had to really stretch yourself at work. What happened?
- Give me an example from your previous job(s) where you had to be creative.
- What was the best mistake you made on the job? Why was it the best?
- Tell me about a time you recognized a problem/area to improve that was outside of your job duties and that you solved without being asked to. What was it, how did you do it?

If your OC values support continued learning and development, you might focus on questions such as:

- What is the last book you read? Would you recommend it to me? Why/why not?
- How do you keep current with what is going on in your field/industry?
- Did you receive feedback on your job performance at your last

position? How often? Was that often enough? Was it helpful? Why?

- What were some areas of development in your last feedback session? What did you think of that and what did you do to improve?

It's no secret that open, honest communication is critical in any organization, but if you want to have a positive OC, it's not just critical, it's an imperative. To evaluate a candidate's communication prowess as it relates to your OC, you might consider questions such as:

- How was communication at your previous company? What would you do to improve it or make it more effective?
- At your previous job, who did you have the most difficult time communicating with and why?
- When was the last time you asked for help at your job? Describe the situation, how did you feel about asking for help?
- What's the most important part of good communication?
- How do you illustrate to someone that you are listening to them?

Finally, if your OC is built around teamwork the following types of questions will help you determine if your candidate's values, philosophies and actions will support your OC:

- Do you feel you are a better individual contributor or a better team player? Which do you prefer?
- When was a time you "took one for the team" even though it wasn't your responsibility?
- When was a time you were thrown work that you were not prepared for? What was the situation? How did you feel about it?
- What's the biggest challenge you faced working in a team

environment? How did you handle it?

- Give me an example of a time you were working with a team/group and one member was not participating/pulling their weight. What did you do?

I am sure you get the basic idea of what we're trying to accomplish with the OC interview. It may be tempting to merely lift these questions out of this book and start using them. After all there are some really good questions here; but beware. Simply using these questions without proper grounding in your organization's OC won't produce the same results because you won't evaluate the responses in a meaningful way that embodies your culture. Use these values questions as a guide to create your own values questions. The point is to specifically design interview questions that will provide realistic insight into the candidate's values and how those align with your organizational values and OC.

How Netflix Focuses On Hiring and Retaining The Right People

Netflix is so passionate about hiring and keeping top talent they practice a motto of "average performance gets a generous severance package." They don't bill themselves as a family. They're a *team*. They boast that they resemble a pro sports team, not a child's recreational team. They believe their leaders are coaches and their job is to hire, develop and "offboard" (read – cut, fire, eliminate, etc.) smartly so they have high performers in every position.

NetFlix also practices what they call the "Keeper Test" which simply means managers periodically evaluate their talent by asking themselves, "Which of my people, if they told me they were leaving in two months for a similar job at a peer company, would I fight hard to keep at Netflix?" For employees who don't make that list, Netflix believes they should receive a generous severance package, so a slot can be opened to find a star for that role.

Netflix also does not tolerate "brilliant jerks", those employees who have lots of talent but that nobody can stand to work with. According to Netflix, "Some companies tolerate them, for us, the cost to teamwork is too high. Diverse styles are fine – as long as person embodies the 9 values". Remember Rome wasn't built in a day and neither was Zappos or Netflix. It takes time to align your hiring practices with your culture. Here are my four must-ask questions to help you identify employees who share your purpose and values and fit your OC:

1. *Why do you want to work at this company and what are your expectations?*

    This question can provide insight into whether the candidate is interested in joining your organization for the right reasons. For example, do they know what it takes to be successful at a start-up, a small company, a large conglomerate, or a for-eign-owned company like your company? Does your company require them to function at a high level with ambiguity? Are they hands-on or do they need a vast staff? Are they ready to get their hands dirty? Are they ready to execute quickly with limited resources? Are they resilient?

    You need to hire people who embrace how your organization operates and the values expected to be upheld.

2. *Who do you look to as a role model and why?*

    A candidate's answer to this question often provides insight into the behavior patterns the candidate respects and emulates.

3. *Which super hero is most like you? Why? What super power do you possess? How do you use it?*

    Everybody has a special talent – something they excel at – a superpower, if you will. That special trait they use when the going gets tough and they need to get results. Make sure you encourage candidates to be open and honest when answering these questions. The candidate's answer will help you get them in the right position where they can make a difference. Making the right assignments and putting together the right team is critical to an organization's success and goes a long way towards ensuring a strong culture fit.

Top talent knows that learning is a lifelong endeavor and they strive to remain intellectually curious throughout their career. Candidates who express a high energy level and intrinsic motivation tend to stay on top of what is happening around them, the organization and the industry. It's a superpower not everyone possesses. When you find someone who is thinking about the world in a way that is bigger than him or herself, that energy is contagious.

4. *How do you rely on others to make you better?*

This question gives candidates the opportunity to show-case a critical characteristic that few possess: self-awareness. In Zappos' world this would be closely related to their value of Be Humble.

Strong, confident candidates know they don't know every-thing; that they aren't the greatest employee in the world. They appreciate the fact that they can learn from others and that others can inspire them to higher levels of performance. They understand their strengths and limitations and can speak to them openly without hesitation. They routinely focus on specific areas where they want to grow, improve, and learn. They spend more time talking about their losses (and what they learned) than their wins. This demonstrates they value collaboration and are comfortable with a transparent work environment.

Hiring is your $1,000,000 decision and with every hire you either reinforce the OC you need to thrive and compete or you chip away at it. During the hiring process be sure to evaluate candidates on both their technical skills and their ability to fit within the culture. Of course, once the candidate is on board, your focus should shift to helping them succeed in their new role. That requires aligning employee development and training.

Aligning Employee Development & Training

Onboarding is "the process of acquiring, accommodating, assimilating and accelerating new team members, whether they come from outside or inside the organization", according to *Onboarding: How to Get Your New Employees up to Speed in Half the Time*, by George Bradt and Mary Vonnegut. Studies have shown that a comprehensive onboarding program pays huge dividends in retaining new hires and in preparing them to make an immediate contribution. A strong onboarding program will achieve a wide range of beneficial outcomes. For example, it will clearly communicate and demonstrate the OC, such as core values and philosophies, while highlighting the purpose of the organization.

So consider broadening your onboarding process to include an overview of your values and philosophies, the history behind each value, the business strategy, the legends and lore of the organization and value the OC brings to the organization. Include specific examples and scenarios to help new hires understand the types of decisions they may be faced with and how you expect them to include the organization's values and philosophies in their actions. Ask other employees or leaders to provide insight into what the values mean to them personally. Your goal is to have the new hires respond on a personal level to the employees' testimonials. If your new hires buy-in to your OC, they will easily reinforce the OC.

Onboarding is only the beginning of the culture immersion process. Organizations that value OC as a competitive advantage view their employee development as an asset, not a liability or another business expense. Leaders, employees, and training facilitators reinforce the OC in every interaction, communication and training course. This ensures employees hear the same message, learn the importance and commitment to the values, and understand how they are expected to **live** the values every day at work.

This approach helps new employees assimilate faster while promoting commitment, dedication and loyalty and increasing engagement. By attracting and retaining top talent that naturally embraces your culture you will reap the benefit of higher performance, greater commitment and stronger team collaboration.

As you'll recall from Chapter 6, there are 6 employee needs that must be met by the organization. Three of the 6 employee needs are: (1) Development - to learn and grow, (2) Belonging – to feel part of something bigger than themselves, and (3) Contribution – to make a difference. When your OC promotes and supports employee learning and development it provides a venue to meet these needs, thus engaging employees at a deeper level and creating commitment. By helping employees increase their skills, build on their strengths and support their values, you enhance their ability to contribute to the organization and conduct themselves in a manner that upholds your OC.

Aligning Performance Management

The onboarding process and during employee training are optimal opportunities to help employees learn how to live the OC. But to truly reinforce the importance of OC, an organization needs a performance management program. Performance management is about cascading the organization's business strategy and organizational objectives to every department and function and to every employee to ensure the organization as a whole is working toward the same goals and objectives. Focusing on performance improvement and learning and development helps create a high performance workforce so the organization is capable of achieving the business strategy.

Performance outcomes will increase quickly when specific objectives are tied to the strategic and operational plan. For example, if the CEO asked for a 3% increase in gross margin, this objective would be cascaded down to every department, team and individual who can influence the increase in gross margin. Employees that achieve the organizational goals are rewarded with favorable reviews and bonuses in line with their performance and contribution to the organization.

Of course, you've probably spotted the main drawback to performance management programs. They focus solely on the results – WHAT was accomplished rather than on the HOW. In other words, did they get those results at the expense of the organization's espoused values and philosophies because the employee's actions, while effective, didn't uphold the OC? The earlier example of Enron and their relentless focus on results not only ignored their desired OC, it undermined it.

It is for this reason that we recommend you review your current performance management program and include a second set of performance measures in the form of Leadership Competencies. Leadership Competencies embody the values and philosophies of the OC and demonstrate the employee's commitment to upholding them.

Leadership Model
& Supporting Competencies

Leaders → **Those They Lead**

	Leadership Competencies (Managers of People at Executive Leadership Team Level)	Front Line Leader Competencies	Individual Contributor Competencies	Admin Support & Technician Individual Contributor Competencies	Shop Floor Competencies
Thinks & Acts Strategically	▶ Business Accumen ▶ Vision & Purpose ▶ Intellectual Rigor	▶ Business Accumen ▶ Vision & Purpose ▶ Intellectual Rigor	▶ Makes Decisions/ Solves Problems	▶ Makes Decisions/ Solves Problems	▶ Makes Decisions/ Solves Problems
Gets Results	▶ Drive for Results ▶ Change & Adaptability ▶ Leveraging Resources	▶ Drive for Results ▶ Change & Adaptability ▶ Leveraging Resources	▶ Drive for Results ▶ Promotes & Champions Changes	▶ Drive for Results ▶ Promotes & Champions Changes	▶ Drive for Results ▶ Job Knowledge
Builds Organizational Capability	▶ Managerial Courage ▶ Holding Self/Others Accountable ▶ Developing & Motivating Others	▶ Managerial Courage ▶ Holds Self & Others Accountable ▶ Develops & Motivates Others	▶ Pursues Personal Development	▶ Pursues Personal Development	▶ Commitment
Demonstrates Leadership Style	▶ Interpersonal Communication Skills ▶ Professional Presence	▶ Interpersonal Communication Skills ▶ Professional Presence	▶ Demonstrates a Collaborative Style	▶ Demonstrates a Collaborative Style	▶ Communication/ Teamwork

Leadership Model

Leadership competencies are customized to reflect the employee's responsibility level within the organization and their ability to make decisions that impact the OC. Leadership competencies provide a dual rating, one for the WHAT, meaning the results and another for the HOW, meaning adherence to the behavioral expectations established by the values and philosophies of the culture. These ratings send the message to all employees that HOW you get results is as important, if not more important, than the results you achieve. In other words, it is not okay to get extraordinary results at the expense of the OC.

This approach helps your organization live by **The OC Equation™** because you aren't simply spouting off about values and philosophies and then rewarding actions that get results but may be contrary to what you said you stand for.

Aligning Internal Communication

Now that you've aligned onboarding with the OC to hire the right people and integrated the OC into learning and development programs, it's time to move on to aligning internal communications with your OC.

Employees have a need to contribute and to belong, as you learned earlier in this book. To meet those employee needs, it is critical to have a culture that promotes openness and dialogue that flows two ways, from the bottom up and the top down. Employees who are included in discussions and decisions that directly affect them are more engaged in the organization. They should be encouraged to talk about what's going on in the organization, the OC, and how their actions support it. Leaders should routinely discuss the OC and share how their decisions support and uphold the OC.

Effective communication is about sending appropriate, informative messages throughout the organization. Employees want to hear those messages from different levels of the organization. For example, employees expect to receive broad messages from top leaders outlining a compelling vision, the mission and the values. Then they expect their immediate leader (supervisor or manager) to help them understand how those messages apply directly to them and how they will be affected.

Strong communication that supports and reinforces your OC includes both sending messages and listening. Ongoing dialogue through a variety of channels reinforces your messages and your OC through repetition and a heightened understanding of expectations (performance and behavioral).

Aligning Rituals and Routines

The rituals and routines of an organization encompass the consistent behaviors and actions of people that indicate what acceptable behavior is and is not. These rituals and routines help establish the expectations in given situations and what is valued by leadership.

Routines may include things such as meetings and gatherings that employees do routinely that bring them together and build comradery. One of my clients fully committed to their OC and a vital component of building their team and ensuring strong communication, collaboration and recognition involves what they call – Third Thursday. This is an opportunity for the entire team to come together and celebrate their successes and accomplishments of the prior month over snacks and beer (or another beverage). They also routinely host client "launch" parties to celebrate the successful launch of a client's project where employees of both companies come together to celebrate and to continue building strong relationships. The rituals and routines your organization engages in reinforce your culture. Is it reinforcing your desired OC or something else? If the answer is "something else", it's time to reevaluate and reenergize.

Aligning Technology

Today's organizations are experiencing an unprecedented evolution of technology and an explosion of capabilities that can be offered to stakeholders. Things are changing so fast many organizations are struggling to keep up. Technology is another opportunity to reinforce your OC by effectively facilitating work and supporting your values and philosophies through proper investment in both hardware and software.

Look at the hacker attacks on Sony Entertainment. Sony knew their systems were vulnerable to attack, according to many news sources, and that their employees' personal data could be at risk. Yet they took no serious steps to proactively upgrade their technological capabilities. What message does that send about their values and how they view their employees?

Although OC appears to be a "soft" skill rather than a technical competency such as technology, it nevertheless is critical to a high performance organization. Don't overlook technology and how that technology is used in reinforcing your OC.

Putting It All Together

Actions speak louder than words – in communication and in OC. If your internal actions are contrary to your espoused OC, employees and other stakeholders will believe your actions and those actions will dictate your OC. That's why **The OC Equation™** uses actions as the multiplier. Your stated values and philosophies are useless if they are not backed-up with visible actions demonstrating your commitment to a strong, positive culture that takes care of both employee needs and the organization's needs.

The OC Equation™ in Action

1 You can't extract another organization's OC and expect to get the same results.

2 To create a sustainable, competitive advantage, the OC has to become part of the organization's DNA – not just another "program".

3 Hire, reward and fire based on your OC to sustain it.

4 Align your performance management system with your OC.

5 Use your organization's legends and lore to communicate and reinforce your OC.

Chapter 10

Living & Projecting Your OC to the World

"He that walketh with wise men shall be wise: but a companion of fools shall be destroyed". Proverbs 13:20

"You become like those with whom you partner"
~ John Maxwell

In March 2014, I began working with an organization that desperately needed HR expertise, focus and guidance, although the CEO loathed the very idea of HR. The organization was a mess. Their guiding value and philosophy, albeit unwritten, was to make money at any and all costs. Although a shrewd businessman, at times the CEO was a complete lunatic. His actions were often inconsistent. He was hot headed, made impromptu decisions and played favorites. In addition, he was self-centered, arrogant and unpredictable with little to no loyalty to anyone or anything – except maybe the financial statement.

He was the kind of leader that employees loathed and feared, mainly because he had a nasty habit of summarily firing anyone he didn't like – even if he "loved" them yesterday. His actions drove fear and mediocrity into the organization resulting in a team of employees who did just enough to get by – no more, no less. Employees generally spent their time trying to figure out how to get as much as possible from the organization before the CEO decided it's their day to go (be fired). With these values, philosophies and actions, why wouldn't the employees be on the ready – they weren't valued and they knew it.

Although he had this erratic behavior, the CEO was nonetheless a savvy businessman as evidenced by his "success" and position and the dynamic growth of his organization.

When I started working with his organization, I had high hopes that I could do what no other HR person had been able to do - change him. I had aspirations that if I demonstrated how treating employees with respect and dignity could earn him an even higher return, he would come around and change his ways. Was I ever wrong!

All this came to a head one day when the CEO discovered through the grapevine that an employee was rumored to have threatened someone he knew. The CEO went into a rage. He was indignant. He called a meeting with HR, the Chief Information Officer, the Safety and Environmental Manager and the VP of Operations. He wanted the young man fired immediately - no investigation into the allegation, no consideration for the fact that this alleged incident happened almost 10 years earlier when the employee was only 18 years old and no consideration for the fact that he had been a model employee with no issues for almost a year. Luckily for the young man, he was on vacation the day of the CEO's tirade allowing cooler heads to prevail and conduct a thorough investigation into the allegations. Another major factor was the fact that the wife of the VP of Operations adored this young man and was able to use her influence to convince the CEO to back down on his initial decision to fire him.

A few weeks later, while I was out of the office, there was a blowup between two employees and their supervisor, whom they reviled. One of the employees complained to the CEO who decided to fire the supervisor since he also didn't like her. He ordered an HR assistant to fire the supervisor. Ironically, the HR assistant had been on the chopping block a few weeks earlier when the CEO decided she wasn't valuable to the organization.

Once I learned of this incident, it became clear, I could no longer work with this organization. My values and philosophies simply were not in alignment with theirs and I feared that my continued association with him, and what I saw as his unethical behavior, would taint HR Solutions by Design by going against our organization's OC diminishing our reputation in the marketplace. In other words, his external practices were out of alignment with my organization's OC.

Not all customers or clients are a "right" customer or client for our organization. Take time to evaluate their values and philosophies and compare those to your organization's values and philosophies. The closer the match, the higher the probability you can have a meaningful, lasting partnership.

As John Maxwell, the esteemed author of *The 21 Irrefutable Laws of Leadership,* puts it, "You become like those with whom you partner. Choose your partners for many of the same reasons a leader chooses his or her inner circle. Choose those who add value to you and can benefit from you. Both leaders and organizations should see improvement for having entered into partnership".

The heart of leading an organization based on **The OC Equation** is to continuously monitor every aspect of your organization's activities to evaluate, examine, reinforce and preserve your OC.

When you, as a leader, understand and embrace your values, both your internal and external sphere of influence will recognize that your talk and your walk are in sync. Espoused values and actions, both internally and externally, will align creating an environment where employees feel stability, purpose and a sense of pride, even during times of significant change, such as when there is restructuring, downsizing, growth, acquisition, mergers, or market fluctuations.

In earlier chapters you learned how to identify your values and philosophies and nourish internal actions that would allow your organization to live its values and philosophies creating a powerful, engaging OC that inspires commitment and performance. Now it's time to consider how your OC translates into your external partnerships and the image those partnerships convey to the world.

Aligning Your External Practices With Your OC

Common questions asked during this phase of the assessment include: Do the people you do business with uphold your values and philosophies? Are your external partnerships consistent with what you say you value? Is your OC supported and reflected through those you align and interact with including external stakeholders, board members, customers, suppliers, media sources, and vendors? Do your products and services reflect your values and philosophies?

Case in Point: In late 2014, Whole Foods, the self-proclaimed "healthiest grocery store in America", launched their *Values Matter* campaign. You can check it out here: https://www.youtube.com/watch?v=5DCow4J-pDE. Through this campaign, they wanted their customers to know what is truly important to them as an organization and what they are committed to providing. Their values include partnerships that support and reinforce responsible fishing, farming and ranching practices. This campaign is designed to connect with their customers by only partnering with suppliers who share their values for sustainable farming and ranching, ethical trade, fair trade practices and healthy living and they articulate that commitment through the tagline – "Value is inseparable from values".

Then they back up these values and philosophies with actions - they don't buy organic products from farmers and ranchers who engaged in questionable farming practices and they don't short-change farmers from other countries on fair pricing for their goods. These practices don't make them the least expensive grocery store, but if you share their values, you shop there in support of a cause you truly care about.

During this phase of the OC assessment, you'll identify and recognize the image your leaders, employees and your brand project outside the organization. You'll evaluate the message sent by your logo, corporate symbols, external rituals and routines, external symbols, the location(s), design and even appearance of your headquarters and other offices. You'll examine the image your leaders portray, and how employees' dress and demeanor affect stakeholder perceptions. You'll also evaluate any external marketing collateral, public relations and advertising campaigns, community activities, charitable giving and other activities in light of your OC. Be sure to also audit your purchase orders, proposals, agreements, warranties and follow-up with clients, vendors and other external stakeholders as well.

Case in Point: In 2007, Mars Petcare featured singer-songwriter Jewel on the cover of their internal employee newsletter. It was exciting to have such a well-known figure featured on the cover, until someone pointed out the fact that the picture featured her in a low cut blouse that seemed inconsistent with Mars' values and philosophies. Once the controversy hit, the cover was no longer about Jewel, Mars Petcare or compassion for our 4-legged friends, it was about sexuality and the unintended message sent to employees and their families. It became a question of Mars' values, which they articulate as the Five Principles and which includes Quality, Responsibility, Mutuality, Efficiency and Freedom, and their wholesome image.

These principles (values) are so engrained into the Mars culture that they provide the following explanation to all internal and external stakeholders: "*We at Mars share special values about our company and the way it should be run. These values — our Five Principles — set us apart from others, requiring that we think and act differently towards our associates, our brands and our business. These principles have always been demanding and are an essential part of our heritage. We believe they are the real reason for our success; they keep us true to ourselves at times of growth and guide us reliably when we are challenged.*"

Tiger Woods lost many sponsors, including Gatorade, AT&T, Accenture, and watchmaker Tag Heuer following revelations of his infidelity and subsequent divorce from Elin Nordegren because his conduct did not reflect the values and philosophies they wanted to portray to external stakeholders.

Gatorade, who is part of the PepsiCo family, is committed to upholding the espoused values and philosophies of PepsiCo as stated below:

PepsiCo Values & Philosophy

Our Values & Philosophy are a reflection of the socially and environmentally responsible company we aspire to be. They are the foundation for every business decision we make.

Our Commitment

We are committed to delivering sustained growth through empowered people acting responsibly and building trust.

What It Means
Sustained Growth

Sustained growth is fundamental to motivating and measuring our success. Our quest for sustained growth stimulates innovation, places a value on results, and helps us understand whether today's actions will contribute to our future. It is about the growth of people and company performance. It prioritizes both making a difference and getting things done.

Empowered People

Empowered people means we have the freedom to act and think in ways that we feel will get the job done, while adhering to processes that ensure proper governance and being mindful of company needs beyond our own.

Responsibility and Trust

Responsibility and trust form the foundation for healthy growth. We hold ourselves both personally and corporately accountable for everything we do. We must earn the confidence others place in us as individuals and as a company. By acting as good stewards of the resources entrusted to us, we strengthen that trust by walking the talk and following through on our commitment to succeeding together.

Gatorade evaluated Tiger's behavior in terms of the image it projected to the world and decided that upholding their values and philosophies and living their OC was most important. They prematurely abandoned their multi-million dollar marketing campaign centered on Tiger Woods as their celebrity endorser rather than lose credibility and trust with their customers.

As the Tiger Woods situation illustrates, organizations may need to dump a celebrity spokesperson to protect their OC. At times even stronger action may be required, as happened with the Baltimore Ravens in 2014 when they decided to cut Ray Rice from the team after allegations of spousal abuse. Then, in a move designed to align their values with the values of their fans, the Ravens offered fans the opportunity to exchange their Ray Rice jerseys for any other Baltimore Ravens player's jersey free of charge! More than 7,000 fans took advantage of the offer costing the Baltimore Ravens over $100,000. But the message from the Ravens (and their fans) was clear: Ray Rice's actions are not consistent with our values and we must act in accordance with what we truly believe regardless of the financial impact to the business. You see, you simply cannot separate your actions from your beliefs. You can separate what you **say** you believe from you actions, but your actions will always betray any hint of inconsistency.

Is What You See, What You Get?

During his 20 year tenure as CEO of the United Way, William Aramony worked tirelessly to combine a smattering of charitable organizations from across the country into one unified organization with a common mission – the United Way. He recruited artist Saul Bass to design a new logo for the United Way - a cupped hand with an arching rainbow. The now much-recognized, iconic symbol was intended to depict the mission and vision of the United Way as "the hand of the United Way bringing hope to people."

In 1995, William Aramony was jailed for defrauding the organization of millions of dollars. He took much needed money that could have been used by the charity to fulfill its mission and vision to enhance his lavish lifestyle and that of his mistresses. His actions also irreparably harmed the United Way, because thousands of employees from all walks of life who had pledged millions of dollars to help those less fortunate found the actions of the United Way's leader did not live up to their values and philosophies and violated their trust in the charity.

While the United Way's reputation has been somewhat restored over the past 20 years, the fact remains that there are those in the public that still don't donate their hard earned money to the organization because they don't trust the organization to be good stewards of it.

In addition to actual monetary donations, the United Way suffered for years to attract and retain top talent – after all, who wants to work somewhere loathed by the public and where they are embarrassed to mention their organization's name?

Your logo, brand, practices and rituals are all reflective of your beliefs and your very existence is dependent on living your OC both internally and externally. What OC is your organization projecting to the world? When assessing your OC, examine what is seen and felt by those outside the organization with the objective of ensuring what you are projecting is consistent with your OC. While living your OC through actions takes more than an image, the image you portray outside the organization needs to be consistent with your values and philosophies because disconnects can have a huge impact on how employees view your organization and whether they are willing to commit and engage in the work of your organization.

For example, if you say you value sustainability and yet your organization throws away millions of pounds of paper and other refuse annually, there is a disconnect between the image you are trying to portray and your actions. Both customers and employees will see these discrepancies and may become disillusioned by the image you outwardly portray, ultimately rejecting you for another competing company that actually lives up to their promises. While this has always been a concern for organizations, it is especially important when interacting with the millennial generation who research organizations and what they stand for and how they act.

Tips for Strengthening the Alignment

1. Align Your Organization's Name with Your OC. "A rose by any other name would smell as sweet." It's a famous quote from William Shakespeare, but in today's competitive world of work, there's actually a lot in a name. Make sure your name reflects who you are as an organization and what you stand for. For example, in 2012 Domino's Pizza decided it was time to drop the "pizza" from their name and simply become Dominos to better reflect who they are as an organization and what they want to be known for to their customers. In February 2015, they launched their new marketing campaign to the public. Check it out here: http://www.ispot.tv/ad/7xnm/dominos-name-change.

2. Determine If Your Organization Symbols Truly Reflect Your OC. Let's take a couple of journeys. Journey 1 - Imagine walking through the front door of a polished glass and mirrored office building on the corner of a bustling downtown city block. People are dressed in formal business attire including Armani suits and Ferragamo shoes and carrying designer briefcases as they walk past trendy coffee shops and flower stands selling loose roses and other fresh-cut flowers. As you approach the reception desk across the wide marble floor you notice a set of clocks noting multiple time zones around the globe. A woman wearing a suit matching lipstick and a cordless headset directs visitors and phone calls with ease and precision. A uniformed security agent stoically observes the passersby periodically giving directions. You enter the elevator through brass-trimmed door opens, when the elevator stops and the door open, you find yourself in a posh reception area with cherry paneling and a lighted logo of the company in front of you. To your left is a glassed conference room with a long marble topped conference table and a glassed view of the city from 20 stories high.

Journey 2 – Now, imagine you've just arrived home after a long, hard day at work only to discover you forgot to pick up something for dinner and there's nothing in the house to eat. Reluctantly you decide to go out for a quick bite.

Arriving at the restaurant, you enter the wide parking lot and quickly find a parking place. Crossing what seems like a massive lot, you enter the building through a small entryway with automatic glass doors that open into a waiting area where other people are standing. Scanning the scene and determining the shortest line, you scurry over and wait patiently to place your order. While waiting, you gaze at the menu posted on the wall along with enticing pictures of various food options. Looking around, you observe a sticky, semi-clean linoleum floor, several booths and tables securely bolted to the floor and a colorful play area for children. When it's finally your turn to order, the cashier messes up your order and calls a manager, who arrives with a heavy bundle of keys, to correct the mistake so she can start over.

So, based on the symbols presented, where have we been? It wouldn't be surprising to learn that our first journey took us to a major corporate headquarters and the second journey landed us at McDonald's or

Huddle House for dinner.

How is it that we understand so much from these brief descriptions of imaginary journeys? That's easy – it's the symbols represented in those descriptions. Symbols are powerful, physical indicators of organizational life and OC. We know that these are different places, with different values and philosophies by the symbols they use to depict who they are and what they value. We can surmise a lot about each organization through the inferences drawn from the objects we encounter (mirrored, glass buildings, heavy etched glass doors, brass elevators, marbled conference tables, cash registers, linoleum floors, and secured booths and tables).

The employees and customers in the two places are also symbolic. For example, we would not be surprised to find a high school student or young college student in a polyester uniform working in the fast-food environment. Nor would we be surprised to find that he/she lacks self-confidence and sometimes makes mistakes. As customers or clients, we tend to match our expectations of performance, behavior and results or outcomes to the surroundings we encounter where the behavior occurs.

In a fast-food environment for example, the symbols tell us that the young worker has a limited set of responsibilities and that his/her job requires a limited amount of knowledge, skill and ability. We know it by the pictures on the buttons of her cash register that match the menu board and the fact that the manager must be called and use his/her keys correct the cashier's mistake.

The symbols in the lobby of the corporate headquarters – including a receptionist in a tailored suit – depicts someone with higher level responsibilities and competence. The smooth technology symbolized in her cordless headset, the appearance of the uniformed security guard and the ease with which she directs visitors are all symbols of the size and buzz of the corporation, and the corporate contributions of her position.

The physical symbols used in an organization integrate feeling, thought, and action into common shared expectations, according to Anat Rafaeli and Monica Worline in the "Handbook of Organizational Culture and Climate". They reflect basic and shared values or assumptions.

Symbols influence behavior by prompting members of the shared community to internalize the values and norms of the community. Based on those symbols, people act out the roles in which they are placed and their awareness of those roles as represented by the symbols present. In addition, symbols also facilitate employee and customer communication and expectations about what to expect in the realm of organizational interaction. Symbols provide a frame of reference to facilitate both behaviors and conversation and present a shared way of getting things done that integrate feelings, thoughts, and behavior into a shared code of conduct.

By aligning your organization's symbols with your OC, you ensure they reflect your organization's ideals in a manner consistent with your values, philosophies, beliefs and actions.

3. **Align The Location, Design and Appearance of Your Organization with Your OC.** Does your OC embrace a conservative tone, a trendy tone, a power tone, or something else? In Nashville, Tennessee, power players look for downtown offices. However, if your OC tends to be trendier and you want to convey an image of innovation and "hipness" – you might consider locating your organization in the Gulch, an upscale off-shoot of downtown Nashville. The point is, the location of your organization makes a statement about your image and what you value. Your satellite office locations and retail stores are physical symbols of your OC.

4. **Align Your Leadership with Your OC** – Your leaders set the tone. The image they project will affect how your organization is

perceived internally by employees and externally by customers or investors. If a leader's image is not consistent with the organization's values and philosophies your OC will mirror that inconsistency.

5. Pay Attention to Employee Appearance Expectations. – Your employees are the face of your organization to clients, customers, board members, suppliers, or other stakeholders. Align their dress or uniforms to your OC to ensure their appearance exemplifies your values and philosophies.

6. Align Your Marketing Collateral and Other PR Events with Your OC. – Your marketing, advertising and other public relations activities should all be designed to reflect your OC through image and perception. Ensure your marketing and ad agencies understand, embrace and commit to your OC before they launch campaigns, otherwise it could be a costly mistake – internally and externally. For example, consider the quick retreat by Go Daddy during the 2015 Super Bowl. Their ad agency decided to mock the beloved Budweiser Clydesdale ads with an ad depicting a lost puppy that was shipped off by its owner to a puppy mill. No doubt Go Daddy wants to be seen as innovative, trendy and hip, but this ad crossed the line with the values of the Super Bowl audience requiring a hasty retreat.

Looking at this situation you may think, they didn't violate any of their core values with this ad, and you're probably right, but they would have violated "Take care of the customer above all else" had they not pulled it from the rotation because their customers rejected it.

7. Align Your Causes with Your OC. – Today's millennial generation is concerned about helping others and standing for something bigger than themselves, so your organization's community activities are an outward symbol of your organization's OC. Be sure to evaluate the causes you support in terms of your values and philosophies to ensure there's alignment and consistency.

The OC Equation™ in Action
1 Evaluate how your OC is portrayed to the world – is it consistent with what happens inside the organization?
2 Your OC is your brand – align it and protect it.
3 Be aware of the message your symbols portray to the external world.
4 Don't forget even the actions of your geography and buildings reflect your OC.
5 When aligned and protected, OC can be a formidable competitive advantage.

Chapter 11

You've Got It – Now How Do You Keep It - Sustaining Your OC

"Engaging the hearts, minds, and hands of talent is the
most sustainable source of competitive advantage"
~ Greg Harris, Quantum Workplace

By virtue of the fact that you're reading this book and are interested in creating an OC that's a competitive advantage – you're ABNORMAL! "Normal" organizations give little to no serious thought to what they believe, what their values and philosophies are or what their actions say about their values and philosophies. While they may recognize there is a "culture" in their organization, they don't truly understand how or why it formed and the impact it has on results. In this chapter we will explore the typical elements that make up an organization and how intentional actions can reinforce and sustain your OC using The OC Equation™.

Making a Difference

What is it in a workplace that actually engages employees to go above and beyond the "norm" to do the right thing rather than just the quick or easy thing? Done right, the answer to that question is your organizational culture (OC). But done wrong, your OC will demotivate employees driving out top talent and leaving mediocrity in its wake, making it even more difficult to compete in today's marketplace.

For many leaders, OC and engagement comes down to the age

old question of which came first – the chicken or the egg? Does high engagement come first and then a winning OC or does a winning OC come first, followed by high engagement? To be a sustainable competitive advantage, your OC must come first. Why? Because it's easy to do the right thing when things are going well, but the true character of your organization and your employees is discovered when things get tough – the market drops, a product launch fails, or a recession hits.

When things get tough, a strong, positive OC keeps employees focused and working together. It builds loyalty and engages employees to work together to overcome obstacles, create value and build the brand.

Organizations that haven't built an OC based on true values and ingrained it into the organization's DNA, will find their employees lose focus, build silos, which results in employees running in all different directions, making individual decisions that best suit their individual values and philosophies and desired outcomes. Your organization will be stratified at the very time it most needs to be unified resulting in wasted time, money and other precious resources.

Which OC is Right for Your Organization?

Read the business headlines and you will see different bloggers and authors touting the need for any number of "cultures" in your organization, including innovation, accountability, engagement, hiring, ethical, trust, clan, adhocracy, hierarchy, market, customer service and the list goes on. But the fact is, there is no such thing as a "Customer Service Culture" you either care about customers because of your values and philosophies or you don't. Another example is a culture of "integrity". If you say you have a culture of integrity and then your actions, hiring, firing and rewarding, demonstrate something less ethical, you don't have a culture of integrity.

You don't need and will never have a single defining culture. The fact that your organization, supported by your OC, is dynamic and flexible is the very thing that allows your employees to do the "right thing" at the right time to support both your organization and your customer's needs. In other words, you can have both a culture of trust and a culture of innovation; you can have a culture of accountability and a culture where employees are considered your greatest asset. They aren't and should never be mutually exclusive.

For example: Let's assume your organization's values include accountability, integrity and innovation. Let's also assume that you've set up excessive policies, procedures and rules that dictate virtually every action to be taken by an employee. Why would employees look for innovative ways to do things? Why would they do the "right thing" for a customer, other employees or the organization if they perceive that the "right thing" is outside the policy? In this example, your actions of establishing a huge bureaucracy essentially tells employees that you don't trust them to either think for themselves (innovation) or do the right thing (accountability). Given that message, they won't, because when employees are focused to simply follow the rules and cease to think there is no motivation to take on the burden of responsibility and accountability for their actions – they are simply doing what they are told. You can tell if you have this type of OC if you hear comments from both leaders and employees such as:

- Sorry, we can't do that, it's against our policy.
- They're having issues with the billing system.
- Any sentence that starts with THEY:
    o They can't get the invoices right.
    o They have meter issues.
    o They don't pay us to think.
    o They won't let us do that.
- It's not my pay grade.
- It must be your problem.
- We're way too busy.
- It's the way we've always done it.

Your OC in Action

Recently, I was exchanging emails on a Saturday afternoon with a client who has a stated value of work/life balance. As we were conversing, she approved an expenditure but asked that I not send the information to her employees until Monday morning because she didn't want to impose on their free time and create a perceived expectation that employees are expected to answer email on nights and weekends.

Wow, that's someone living their OC through the expectations she sets and the actions she takes. And that's a good thing because a recent study suggests that employees are "dying" of email. A 2012 survey by the Center for Creative Leadership found that 60% of smartphone-using professionals keep in touch with work for a full 13.5 hours per day, and then spend another 5 hours juggling work email each weekend. That's 72 hours a week of job-related contact!

Another survey of 1,000 workers by Good Technology, a mobile-software firm, found that 68% checked work email before 8 a.m., 50% checked it while in bed, and 38% "routinely" did so at the dinner table. Fully 44% of working adults surveyed by the American Psychological Association reported that they check work email daily while on vacation—about 1 in 10 checked it hourly. It only gets worse as you move up the ladder. According to the Pew Research Center, people who make more than $75,000 per year are more likely to worry that their phone makes it impossible for them to unplug and enjoy some "down time".

When assessing behavior and OC, you need to be sure you understand employee and leader behavior and what's driving their actions, because whatever is driving their actions may either support and reinforce your OC or undermine it.

Case in Point: Traveling from New Jersey one week, my flight was delayed. Sitting in the terminal, I noticed the woman next to me pulled out two phones and a laptop to get some work done. She had one phone for personal use and a second phone for business provided by her employer. "It's my leash," she joked. "They jerk my chain and I am expected to respond." As I was talking to her she elaborated, "If some-body from work emails me on Friday at 10 p.m., they're ticked off if I don't respond in five to ten minutes." Naturally that comment piqued my interest, so I asked if she ever turned it off and disconnected. She stared at me as if I had two heads and horns, shook her head in annoy-ance, and said "My boss would kill me".

Clearly this woman was behaving in a manner consistent with the OC of the organization and was complying out of fear. But compli-ance and fear will only result in employees doing just enough to get by. In the absence of true engagement, there is no loyalty or "going the extra mile". So, in these situations leaders need to ask themselves, are employees acting out of fear and compliance or out of loyalty and com-mitment? The answer will provide insights into your true OC.

Sustaining Your "Desired" OC

Your OC only has staying power as long as your leaders and employ-ees - those with influence – live and breathe it. You've likely heard the old sayings "what gets measured gets done" and "what gets rewarded gets repeated". These statements are true in business and in sustaining your OC. Not only must leaders "say" the right things, they must act in a manner that consistently demonstrates their support and belief in the organization's values and philosophies. This means every action – not just a few, selective actions that fit the moment. Otherwise, leaders will erode trust and destroy the desired OC.

Sustaining your OC takes commitment, hard work, diligence, intentionality and consistent application throughout the entire employee lifecycle. Hire wisely, onboard and assimilate quickly, train/mentor often and cut bait when needed. The point is, with every interaction throughout the employee lifecycle comes an opportunity to either support or erode your desired OC. It is, literally, what you make it.

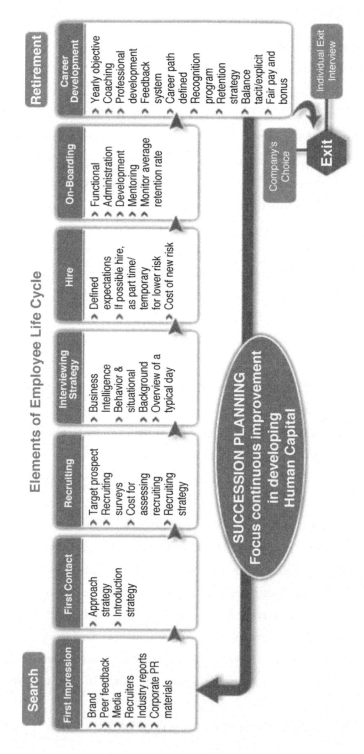

Elements of Employee Life Cycle

Search

First Impression
> Brand
> Peer feedback
> Media
> Recruiters
> Industry reports
> Corporate PR materials

First Contact
> Approach strategy
> Introduction strategy

Recruiting
> Target prospect
> Recruiting surveys
> Cost for assessing recruiting
> Recruiting strategy

Interviewing Strategy
> Business Intelligence
> Behavior & situational
> Background
> Overview of a typical day

Hire
> Defined expectations
> If possible hire, as part time/ temporary for lower risk
> Cost of new risk

On-Boarding
> Functional
> Administration
> Development
> Mentoring
> Monitor average retention rate

Retirement

Career Development
> Yearly objective
> Coaching
> Professional development
> Feedback system
> Career path defined
> Recognition program
> Retention strategy
> Balance tacit/explicit
> Fair pay and bonus

Company's Choice

Individual Exit Interview

Exit

SUCCESSION PLANNING
Focus continuous improvement in developing Human Capital

Making it Happen

Your organization's OC has never been more visible and important than it is today. Today, organizations face greater scrutiny than at any time in history. The advent and explosion of social media ensures that organizational decisions are immediately available to be publically scrutinized, debated and exposed. What may have once been considered internal or private matters can now instantly blow up into public relations nightmares, exposing the organization to not only embarrassment but litigation and even loss of market share.

Case in Point: Recently a global financial services company was embroiled in a series of events that damaged their reputation with the public and eroded trust among their employees. When the organization decided they needed to implement a turnaround plan they decided to start by building a sustainable values-driven OC. To make that happen, they focused on three key principles to ensure the program's success.

1. The involvement of engaged leaders to drive the change and be accountable for the results.
2. Processes, policies and systems that support actions that overtly demonstrate the commitment to the desired OC.
3. Measurable results tracked closely both internally and externally.

The organization also implemented a learning and development program focused on change management principles to ensure employees at all levels were willing and able to "live" the organization's values and philosophies. The focus was on making employees aware of the reasons for the change, actively engaging the employees in the process by helping them discover a personal reason why supporting the new OC was important to them, and providing the tools and resources needed to empower employees to live and promote the new OC through their everyday actions.

Once the learning and development was in place, they began aligning their policies, processes and systems with their values and philosophies and to drive the desired OC, including performance management, talent management, reward and recognition and accountability. They also launched a culture assessment to track progress and measure results. At the end of the 5-year transformation the organization noted their public reputation had improved, the leadership team was aligned and committed to the OC and were more respected and trusted, and employees were more engaged and committed to the organization's OC, vision and success.

What would have been an internal decision with internal actions that only employees would have been aware of, became, in today's world of instant communication of those decisions and actions, a nightmare for this financial services organization. Faced with a serious public relations problem and a damaged reputation, they made a major effort to "fix" their OC and ensure it was maintained. Below are steps that your organization can use to maintain OC.

Getting Started – Building a Sustainable HR Infrastructure

You learned in earlier chapters how to create values and philosophies that multiply actions. To sustain your OC, take another look at how your organization does things. Review every policy, process and system used in your organization to evaluate how they're used and the behaviors they drive in light of those values and philosophies. In other words, do the actions of your organization support and reinforce your desired OC?

Where there are inconsistencies, consider changes.

Strategy Development

Creating, implementing and sustaining an OC doesn't happen in an HR vacuum. Many organizations create business strategies paying little attention to their desired OC and the HR strategies needed to ensure success, perhaps assuming that employees' attitudes, beliefs and actions will just naturally follow.

Like OC, there is no right or wrong strategy; only an effective or ineffective strategy. Let's look at several very effective, albeit different strategies that are supported by OC and actions.

Strategy and Culture in Action – Apple and Google take pride in their strategic focus on innovation. Employees are expected to think creatively and then to attempt to implement their creative ideas. Not all ideas work, but that's not the point. The point is to reward employees for taking risks. It all pays off with improved morale, increased work output and the occasional marketable new gadget or program. Both pride themselves on their strategic focus on innovation. Employees are empowered to think and act differently, outside the box so to speak.

If your organization values innovation, as does Apple and Google, then your actions must reward employees for both thinking creatively and then actually implementing those creative ideas. For example, at Google they practice what they call *20% Time* where employees are allowed up to one day per week to work on a creative idea they are passionate about. These ITO (Innovation Time Off) programs empower employees to explore and be creative, which can improve morale, increase work output and at time produce a game changer.

Wal-Mart, on the other hand, makes no bones about the fact that their business model focuses on being the low cost alternative in their markets. To keep customer costs low, they must keep internal costs low. Because of this philosophy, they value efficiency over innovation and policies and processes are designed to reward actions focused on conserving resources and money – both of which protect their ability to execute their strategy. In terms of OC, this translates into clearly defined job roles and responsibilities where employees know exactly what they are supposed to be doing.

No one can argue that all three organizations are hugely successful in executing their respective strategies, yet all three have vastly different OCs. Ultimately, your organization's success implementing its business strategy will be directly related to how well your OC aligns with that strategy. Let's look at some practical tips for aligning culture and strategy.

Tips for aligning culture and strategy:

1. Identify and focus on ACTIONS (behaviors) that will lead directly to desired outcomes.
2. Evaluate those ACTIONS against your stated values and philosophies – are they congruent? If not, proceed with caution or change either your actions or values.
3. Implement business and OC metrics and make outcomes both observable and measurable.
4. Lead by example – it's up to you to model OC expectations.
5. Realign your reward systems with your OC and desired ACTIONS.
6. Ensure people see a clear connection between their ACTIONS and the desired OC.
7. Communicate organizational values and philosophies while focusing on the strategy.

Tactical Components for aligning culture and strategy:

- Select the strategic direction, goals and objectives.
- Determine which ACTIONS (behaviors) are necessary to achieve the goals and objectives.
- Identify the OC attributes in your organization that will reinforce those ACTIONS (behaviors) such as stories (legends and lore), key relationships, rituals and ceremonies that influence internal and external behavior.
- Identify the OC attributes in your organization that may create barriers to positive ACTIONS (behaviors) needed to achieve those results.

- Determine ACTIONS (behaviors) that need to change to achieve results AND reinforce your OC.
- Ensure leaders model and promote expectations for performance through OC.

Risk-O-Meter

Is your organization a risk taker or is it risk averse? When asked this question, most leaders say they promote risk taking. But do they really? Risk taking is critical to creating and sustaining an OC where innovation and creativity are valued. But when faced with the possibility and accountability of failure, many leaders lose their confidence resulting in situations where they say one thing but act altogether different.

If you say you value creativity and innovation, then your OC has to support creativity and innovation by encouraging employees to take reasonable risks without fear of reprisal. According to an article by Great Workplace, a recent study conducted by Blessing White found that 41% of employees said their leaders never encouraged them to take risks and 33% said their leaders only sometimes encourage them to take risks. Remember, actions speak louder than words – especially when it comes to OC.

Leaders who truly value innovation and creativity foster healthy risk-taking at the grass roots levels. They recognize the need to overcome their own or others' authoritative style. It also means they need to address indifference and overcome the "that's the way we've always done it" mindset. Leaders committed to sustaining a risk-taking OC, promote innovative ways of working. They know if they don't overcome these challenges, they risk squandering their human capital advantage and losing to their competitors.

Don't worry if you're sitting there thinking "my company's not an Apple and never will be, so why do I need to worry about innovation"? Innovation is not just about coming up with big breakthroughs or industry and life changing ideas. It's also about encouraging innovation and creativity in routine activities. Or, as Wharton professor, George S. Day, says in *Innovation Prowess*: "The organization-driven product or customer-focused breakthrough is innovation with a capital 'I' and new processes and creative work applications are innovation with a little 'i'. Both are important." Does your organization's actions convey a big "I" or a little "I"?

Does your organization balance the need to focus on short term and long-term priorities? If you're consumed with and reward firefighting in the short term, then why would you expect employees to innovate ideas for the long term future? Pressure for productivity and quarterly earnings often takes priority in an organization, but if you want your employees and customers to believe you value innovation and creativity, you have to balance that with more long-term priorities.

For example, say the R&D and Marketing departments disagree on the most effective process for rolling out new products. You're struggling with who should be responsible for generating the next big idea. In an OC that genuinely values innovation and creativity, it's not an either/or scenario – rather both departments would be expected to venture out of their comfort zones and work together to overcome the disruptions and uncertainties. This approach may appear to slow down the process at first, but with practice and commitment, the actions associated with your values and philosophies (your OC) will ultimately encourage and reinforce the expectation that all employees explore new ways of collaborating so as to generate both more big "I"s and little "i"s.

To generate more big "I's" and little "i's" with an OC of innovation and creativity, consider implementing these actions:

- Educate employees on what is meant by innovation, creativity and risk taking.
- Get leaders on board and reward THEM for rewarding risk taking.
- Openly share and celebrate successes – and failures. Celebrate that risk was taken even if it didn't work out as planned. Actively

demonstrate that measured risk is not only acceptable, but celebrated and the learnings pave the way for future success.

- Don't accept poor performance disguised as risk taking. Poor performance is NOT the same thing as risk taking. Did an employee try something different that didn't work out as planned, but the work was solid and delivered with excellence and on time? That's risk taking. Or was the work sub-par, late and technically unsound? That is not risk taking; it's poor performance that must be addressed so it doesn't erode your OC.

- Openly mine for (constructive) conflict by encouraging employees to share different perspectives and viewpoints without fear of reprisal.

- Implement beta testing to try ideas without making a full commitment of resources. Providing a vehicle where employees can test the waters before making a full commitment of time, people and money will continue to reinforce your commitment to risk taking, and will limit your overall exposure.

- Include risk taking as a goal and objective in your performance management program, measure it and then provide rewards based on how well it's implemented and the results achieved. Remember, what gets measured – gets done!

With great risk comes great reward and companies that value risk-taking, tend to be wildly successful, as demonstrated by Apple or Google. But taking risks will only work if the organization's structure supports an OC of risk taking.

Organizational Structure

Organizational structure isn't something most leaders lay awake at night thinking about, but without the right structure to support your OC and your business strategy, you figuratively and literally leave profits on the table.

So, what does it mean to organize?
(No, it's not what you're thinking!)

Organizing is a process of structuring working relationships to leverage your OC (how things get done) to encourage and enhance employees' ability to achieve organizational goals and objectives – and ultimately – the business strategy. In other words, it's a formal system of tasks and reporting relationships that determine how employees effectively utilize the resources available to accomplish their work assignments.

When designing an organizational structure, you've got to make specific decisions about the reporting relationships and tasks expected. It's these decisions that ultimately create the organization's structure.

On the surface this may sound easy – after all, how hard is it to decide who is going to report to whom. But under the surface of those decisions, based on your leaders' values and philosophies, lies the challenge: designing a structure that will support and reinforce your values and philosophies through actions. To perpetuate a strong, positive OC your organizational structure should:

1. Engage employees at all levels reinforcing hard work and mutually beneficial work behaviors and attitudes.
2. Build cohesiveness coordinating activities of individuals, groups, functions and divisions to ensure both efficiency and effectiveness.

The Organizational Environment

Today's world is smaller than ever and the spirit of entrepreneurship has never been greater – especially for millennials who expect to be taken seriously right out of the gate. This ever-changing environment is causing uncertainty and unpredictability which must be tempered with critical communication, agility, flexibility and quick, decisive action.

Given the state of today's business environment, leaders need to develop an organizational structure with the agility and flexibility to speed up decision making while managing unnecessary risk. This is often accomplished by decentralizing authority and empowering employees to make decisions that directly affect them thus encouraging change and innovation.

Structure and Strategy

Different strategies demand different OCs and different structures. For example, an organization with a differentiation strategy aimed at increasing quality often succeeds best in a structure that promotes flexibility and a culture that hires, rewards, and fires for innovation. Apple lives and dies by their differentiation strategy.

Contrast that with an organization's low cost strategy aimed at driving down costs (Wal-Mart). This often calls for a more formal, conservative culture where managers maintain much of the decision making and control.

On the other hand, in organizations supported by a vertical integration or a diversification strategy (Starbucks), flexibility is needed to provide sufficient coordination among business divisions.

Linking and Coordinating

The more complex your organizational structure, the more problems you'll face in linking and coordinating functions, departments and people. Coordination often becomes a problem because each function or department may fragment from the overall organization developing a unique orientation within their own department or group. This is where you constantly revert back to your values and philosophies for a gut check by asking yourself, "Do my actions reinforce and support my espoused values or do they contradict them?"

Organizations striving to manage this fragmentation empower leaders to develop clear lines of authority – the power to make decisions, allocate resources and use resources to achieve the organizational strategy, goals and objectives. This is often accomplished by implementing a chain of command.

Big or Small; Flat or Tall

It's no surprise that the larger an organization becomes, the more likely it is to implement numerous levels of authority. The result is a complex (tall) hierarchy where decisions take time and multiple levels must bless the decision before actions can be implemented. As tall organizations rise, communications often break down, agility is lost and flexibility becomes almost non-existent. Tall organizations usually have complex bureaucracies.

Flat organizations, on the other hand, push decision making to the lowest possible level and employees are empowered to make decisions and drive results with minimal input and oversight. These organizations rely on decentralized authority which tends to improve communications because fewer managers are needed and employees are empowered to recognize and respond to customer needs.

There is no right or wrong structure – only what works for your organization. Edward Deming, the father of the modern quality movement, viewed management as vital to an organization's OC and its success, or lack thereof. His central message to Japan and this country was "that they (management), not employees, were the problem, and that nothing would get better until they took personal responsibility for change".

Hire, Reward and Fire for OC

Your OC and organizational structure can't be maintained unless a conscious decision is made to protect it through who you hire, the behaviors you reward, and the violations on which you fire. This is where so many organizations go astray in attempting to establish or maintain their OC because they tend to emphasize knowledge, skills and abilities over values in the hiring and employment process, leading inevitably to the termination process.

For example, if your organization values employee involvement and empowerment and creates a flat organizational structure to support those values, but hires high level managers who value command and control, it won't take long before your flat, flexible structure is replaced with a complex chain of command and hierarchy.

Other Departments

How do you anticipate your values and philosophies will influence interactions between departments and functions? Do your actions encourage and demand collaboration and teamwork or do they encourage silos and turf wars where resources are scarfed up and protected by a single department rather than shared for the overall effectiveness of the organization? All these outcomes are based on your OC, which is driven by your values, philosophies and actions.

An effective organizational structure supports and maintains your intentional OC – that set of shared values, beliefs, expectations and norms used to achieve desired business results. Your OC is embodied in **The OC Equation™**:

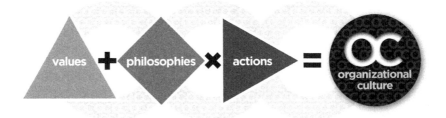

Different structures reinforce different OCs. Tall, hierarchical structures promote little personal autonomy giving rise to OCs where caution, obedience, tradition and authority are emphasized. Flat structures that emphasize decentralization encourage and reinforce cultures that reward creativity, risk taking and personal responsibility. The choice is yours and should be based on what best suits your OC because if you want to sustain an intentional OC make sure your words and actions match.

Standards, Policies, and Guidelines

An organization's policies, procedures, standards and guidelines are the window into your OC because they provide a glimpse into how the organization expects things to get done. While the intention is to provide structure and consistency, companies often have written policies and guidelines in place, but actually do something altogether different in practice. Think about the last time you heard someone say, "Yeah, I know that's what they say, but that's not how it really works!"

The level of guidance can either be broad with a big picture overview of what's expected (guidelines), semi-specific (policies and procedures) or very detailed and specific (procedures and standards). Your OC will naturally dictate what's used. For example, if you have an OC where employees are viewed as adults and it's assumed that the majority will naturally "do the right thing", your OC may dictate you implement broad, overarching guidelines. Conversely, if your OC is more skeptical and tends to believe employees cannot fully be trusted and need detailed expectations, lest they stray, you may opt for a mid-level policy or a detailed, non-negotiable standard. There is no one right or wrong approach; they all have their advantages and disadvantages. No matter what you choose, just make sure it's consistent with what you say you value. Remember, no matter what your OC, it can quickly be eroded unless you purposefully hire, fire and reward to protect it.

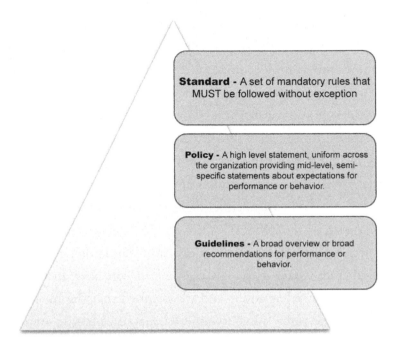

The OC Equation™ offers insight into policies, guidelines and standards. For example, your values provide a broad guideline for behaviors and how decisions are made. Philosophies take it a step further providing detailed examples of how values are expected to be demonstrated through actions, which are the outward manifestation of the actual values and philosophies.

Developing Your Policies and Guidelines

Clients often ask, "How do I create policies that will support the Organizational Culture (OC) I am trying to develop and maintain?"

As with most things cultural, the answer is simple, but not simplistic. Let me give you an example. Recently we worked with a client whose stated objective is to drive a culture of innovation and accountability. But their expense reporting policy did anything but drive innovation and accountability.

In this particular situation the client was hosting a regional conference with employees from several states. They booked a meeting location using a national hotel chain, secured a block of rooms at a discounted price, ordered catering, etc. You know the drill. The meeting space was conveniently located in an area of town that was easily navigated from the airport using either light rail or a hotel shuttle and there were plenty of restaurants and shopping within walking distance. Although the participants and speakers were provided this information, there was no stated policy requiring them to book accommodations at the host facility or forbidding them from selecting accommodations elsewhere.

While booking reservations, we realized that the accommodations at the host hotel were very expensive. Much higher than we were accustomed to so we began looking for other alternatives. With little effort, we found a comparable hotel a mile or so away from the meeting location whose rate was much lower, offering considerable savings for the client. The only catch was, because of distance and safety it would also require use of a rental car. After doing a few calculations, we discovered the combined cost of the hotel and the rental car was still cheaper for the client than booking at the host hotel and taking the "free shuttle". So, we booked the alternate hotel and patted ourselves on the back for being innovative and saving the client money – confident our innovation and accountability had created a win-win situation for all involved.

Ahhh, but it quickly became evident that saving money was not the objective. When expense reports were finalized and sent to the client and they realized we booked a rental car, they summarily refused to honor reimbursement of that expense explaining they would not pay for a rental car in a location that provided a shuttle. Never mind that our accommodations were cost neutral at worst and at best actually saved them money! Their focus was clearly on an "unwritten" policy that no rental car could be used if a shuttle was available. You see, the client trusted us with their most valuable asset – their employees – but they didn't trust us to make good business decisions with their money.

So, let's consider the consequences of this situation in terms of their stated values and philosophies. If the client truly valued innovation and accountability, did their policies and actions reinforce those espoused values? What message did their action send to those involved? What is the likely outcome of these actions in the future?

Focusing on Intent

Whether you use strict policies and standards or overarching guidelines, they can both be effective. But to drive consistency, it's best to begin with what's intended. What are you trying to accomplish with the policy or guideline?

For example, if you have a relocation policy that provides employees with monetary benefits to ensure they remain "whole" when making a move on behalf of the company, the usual intent is to provide the employee with products and services to ease the transition. The intent is not for the employee to profit from the move but to ensure the employee doesn't "lose" money making the move. When leaders and employees understand the intent of the policy (to keep the employee "whole") they can easily consistently surmise the answer to even the oddest questions while maintaining the OC.

Case in Point: An employee is moving from an apartment and asks if the company will pay for the closing costs associated with buying a house. While the relocation policy allows for paying for closing costs for homeowners, it does not allow for closing costs for renters (because there are no closing costs to rent a home). When you understand the intent of the policy, it's an easy answer. The intent of the policy it to ensure employees relocating from another city are kept whole during the move. It is not to provide a profit to employees. Had the renter remained in her/his previous location and decided to purchase a house, closing costs would not have been provided by the company. Therefore, it would be inconsistent to pay for closing costs if the employee decides to buy a house in the new location instead of renting.

When employees aren't informed of the intent of policies and are treated as though they aren't capable of making good decisions using their own critical thinking skills, they stop engaging in innovative activities and being accountable for their decisions. That same attitude applies to vendors, suppliers, or business partners. In the expense account case, there is no way we will ever try to save this client money again if saving them money goes against their "policy". No thinking, no innovation and no accountability – just follow the policies blindly. Are your policies counter-productive to your desired OC and restricting your ability to compete?

Reward and Recognition (R&R) Programs Drive Actions

During our college years most, if not all of us learned from B. F. Skinner that if you want more of a certain behavior – reward it. Employee and organizational behavior are no different. Sustaining your OC requires intentionally rewarding employees who live it all the time, not just when the boss is looking or when a high level leader is visiting; but when there's no one around or when they think no one's paying attention. A reward doesn't necessarily mean monetary rewards, trinkets, dinners, or other such perks. It means showing genuine appreciation for a job well done.

When formal reward and recognition (R&R) programs attempt to appeal to employees through extrinsic rewards, it will likely only work as long as the reward is present. Take away the reward and the behavior ceases. For example, GM is notorious for offering buyers incentives for purchasing a new vehicle. In fact, during the 2008 recession when money was tight and the car market dried up along with GM's revenue, they stopped offering incentives and buyers responded in kind. Extrinsic incentives and rewards only work as long as they are offered. Rewards sometimes work against what you're actually trying to accomplish because people are focused on the reward and not the intent behind the reward.

R&R programs sometimes go astray, rewarding a different behavior altogether. These programs are almost always developed with the best of intentions and it's only later that leaders discover the unintended consequences driving contrary behaviors and actions.

For example, in the early 1990's, Sears and Roebuck Co. was concerned about diminishing profits at their auto centers. Sears introduced what it believed was a cost-cutting, productivity-enhancing incentive plan for their auto mechanics. Using the concept of performance-based pay, they reduced the mechanics' base pay and implemented a piece rate system whereby their mechanics would earn a fixed dollar amount in addition to their base salary for completing jobs within a specified time period. The Service Advisors' pay was also restructured to include a base salary plus commission. Quotas were established for both the mechanics and service advisors. Driven by their sales quotas and piece rate mentality, Sears Auto Centers began overcharging customers for repairs, recommending repairs that weren't needed and even charging customers for work that had not been completed. Needless to say, the consequences proved detrimental to employee morale, customer trust and brand loyalty. After the class action lawsuit, their brand and reputation were almost unrepairable.

Or consider a more mundane example of R&R programs gone awry. Your company develops an R&R program to reward its highest sales person while touting values and philosophies around teamwork and cooperation. While you say you value employees working together and helping each other achieve the business results, your R&R program sends a different message, one that says whoever sells the most wins an all-expense paid vacation to the Bahamas for themselves and their family. What actions and behaviors do you think you will achieve with this particular R&R program?

There is no doubt: what gets rewarded gets repeated. Whether its children, adults or employees: if you want more of a specific behavior or actions, reward it. Just make sure if you want to use OC as a competitive advantage, your words, actions, and rewards send the same messages.

To Sustain your OC, You Have to Live It

Your OC can either be your organization's competitive advantage or it's Achilles' heel. To be effective, your Organizational Culture (OC) must be continually reviewed and reinforced. It's not something you can write on a wall, cover in this year's annual report, tout in a marketing message and then forget. It must be actively evaluated and reevaluated with every decision made. Employees at every level must be trained on what it means to be an employee in your organization, what your values are and the philosophies that explain what's behind those values. They must assimilate into your OC and grow to understand how decisions are made and expected to be made. When they make decisions consistent with your desired OC, they must be rewarded and recognized for upholding the OC even if in the short term it appears to be a less competitive decision.

For example, I have a dear friend who is a business owner with several locations across middle Tennessee. As a Christian, he values honesty and integrity. Having been in business for many years, he owns property in what is today considered high value areas that developers are clamoring to get their hands on. My friend and colleague promised an adjacent business owner that he would sell him several acres of property for $160,000 an acre and he gave his neighbor all year to close the deal. In November 2014, the neighbor came to my friend and reminded him of his promise. Although other real estate in the area had sold for $100,000 more per acre, my friend reiterated to his neighbor that he was committed to the deal they had negotiated as long as it closed by December 31, 2014. There was no written contract, and his daughter, an attorney, assured my friend that his verbal agreement wasn't binding. But in his mind, based on his values of honesty and integrity, the verbal agreement was indeed binding because it was his word. He was committed to living his values, even if in this business deal it meant losing a substantial amount of money.

Sometimes it may seem that to hold to your values, especially when the rest of the world does not, is a stupid idea. But if you want your OC to be a competitive advantage recognized by employees, candidates, customers, and vendors you have to live it all the time.

The OC Equation™ in Action
1 High performing leaders tend to what's important, focusing on priorities and convincing others that those priorities are critical.
2 There are no "right" or "wrong" OCs, just the one that's right for your organization, based on your Values and Philosophies and backed up by your Actions.
3 Hire wisely, onboard and assimilate quickly, train/mentor often and cut bait when needed.
4 Align your business strategy with your OC strategy to ensure your actions support your values and philosophies.
5 To sustain a strong, positive OC, you have to "live" it with every decision and action you take.

Chapter 12

Live Your OC
and Influence Greatness!

"Our influence has less to do with our position or title
than it does with the life we live. It is not about the education we get, but the empowerment we give, that makes a
difference to others" ~ John Maxwell

I t's unavoidable, a leader's values and philosophies will permeate every
aspect of their personal and professional environment influencing and
impacting how the leader views the world, evaluates information, and
make decisions.

If employees understand the leaders' values and philosophies and see
leaders acting in ways that support and reinforce (live) those values and
philosophies, consistent behavior patterns will emerge building confidence among employees that those same patterns will be repeated in
future decisions and actions. The congruency between the values and
philosophies and subsequent supporting actions, as measured through
The OC Equation™, will allow you to build a strong, positive OC
based on trust and loyalty which in turn can translate into high employee
engagement where employees are emboldened to actively engage in the
activities of organization in a way that drives superior performance
based on the belief that future decisions will be assessed and made in a
similar manner.

While understanding the organization's values and philosophies is
an important first step, if employees are encouraged, and even required,

to share, embrace and live the organizational values and philosophies, a unifying OC will take hold. When the OC is strong and positive, greater employee satisfaction and commitment will begin to emerge because repeated behavior patterns can be trusted which will ultimately lead to enhanced performance. As more and more employees accept and buy into the OC, believing it to be beneficial to them as employees, as well as to the health and welfare of the organization, momentum will grow establishing the conditions where the OC can ultimately be leveraged as a competitive advantage.

Now, go forth, create and live your only true competitive advantage – a winning OC that no one else can emulate.

Afterword

Leaders create momentum, followers catch it, and managers help sustain it. But to create momentum, a leader has to be able to inspire others. Living your organizational culture (OC) isn't easy and takes someone willing to create change within the organization. Every sailor knows that you can't navigate a ship that's not moving forward and strong leaders know that you can't change direction unless you create the momentum to initiate forward progress – and that takes the passion of your people.

Momentum creates an environment where anything seems possible, where the future looks bright, problems are viewed as challenges and trouble is seen as but a fleeting moment in time that will pass.

If your team is to gain and sustain the momentum needed to create your true competitive advantage they have to be united around a compelling and inspiring purpose and vision, embrace a set of common, passionately held values and philosophies and possess the courage to live those values and philosophies through their actions.

In Daniel 6: 1-10 in the Bible, we find Daniel struggling to decide if he should retain his position of power in the kingdom by submitting himself to ungodly law or risk losing it to uphold his convictions. Daniel chose to hold firm to his values and philosophies and stand by his convictions. He was ultimately imprisoned and thrown into the lion's den.

Deciding to follow or abandon your values and philosophies might not prove to be as perilous as Daniel's, but it will make an impact on your organization – both in the short and long term. Your values, philosophies and actions will create an OC that will either create or destroy momentum.

Just as in the days of Daniel, living your OC isn't always the easiest path, but it will always be the most meaningful path. **The OC Equation™** is your roadmap to success in sustaining your only true competitive advantage – your people. To live your OC consistently you must:

- Identify what you truly value
- Articulate the philosophies behind those values
- When situations present themselves, carefully weigh your options
- Ask if those options force you to compromise your values
- Seek wise counsel
- Consider the costs
- Make your decision based on your values and philosophies
- Act on your decision swiftly and firmly

Leaders who are respected and revered don't passively react to their organization's OC, they build and sustain their OC based on long held values and philosophies that define not only their leadership but them personally and then back that up with their actions. True leaders sustain relevance because they marry their OC with timeless truth. Is your leadership, and thus your organization, principle centered?

In Psalm 15:1-2, David describes a righteous leader who walks in integrity and gains the respect of others. These verses outline why predetermined values and philosophies, not expediency, are the key to meaningful leadership. John Maxwell puts it best in *The Maxwell Leadership Bible*, "The [principle-centered] leader:

- Possesses integrity
- Does what is right
- Is honest and trustworthy
- Does not gossip

- Does not listen to gossip
- Does no harm to others
- Speaks out against wrong
- Honors others who walk in truth
- Keeps their word even when it costs them
- Isn't greedy to gain at the expense of others
- Takes no bribes against anyone
- Is strong and stable"

In today's society, employees are hungry for leaders who will lead with integrity, who base decisions on something they can hold onto. If you're going to win, not only in the war for talent but in the marketplace, why not be abnormal and base your competitive advantage on something truly unique and sustainable – your Organizational Culture (OC)?

Acknowledgements

I would like to acknowledge the following people who have served as mentors and friends throughout my career – without you and your teachings this book would not have been possible.

Gene Corbett – My lifelong mentor. Everything I learned about human resources and OC, I learned from you. I would not have had the incredible career I've had without your support, faith and teachings. May God bless and keep you always.

Mickey Hanner – The best #2 anyone could ever have! Although you are now top dog in your own right, you were the glue that held everything together when we worked as a team. You taught me the importance of OC and to appreciate and coach employees and leaders at all levels to build and sustain an OC that would ensure the business results and employee engagement.

Steve Bartlett – You helped me put OC in perspective. Learning to appreciate the history, values and philosophies of a great organization and the hard decisions that must be made to live up to the legacy and demonstrate the values and philosophies with every daily decision was key to fully developing The O.C. Equation™. Without your tutelage I may have missed those nuances.

References/Resources

Chapter 1

Culture [Def. 1]. (n.d.). *Merriam Webster Online.* In Merriam-Webster. Retrieved June 12, 2015, from http://www.merriam-webster.com/dictionary/culture.

Watson, T. (2012). *Engagement at risk: Driving strong performance in a volatile global environment.* New York, NY.

Chapter 2

Gallup, Inc. (2013). *State of the American workplace: Employee engagement insights for U.S. business leaders.* Retrieved from http://employeeengagement.com/wp-content/uploads/2013/06/Gallup-2013-State-of-the-American-Workplace-Report.pdf

Chapter 4

Gallup, Inc. (2013). *State of the American workplace: Employee engagement insights for U.S. business leaders.* Retrieved from http://employeeengagement.com/wp-content/uploads/2013/06/Gallup-2013-State-of-the-American-Workplace-Report.pdf

Logan, D., King J., & Fischer-Wright, H. (2011). *Tribal leadership: Leveraging natural groups to build a thriving organization.* New York, NY: Harper Business.

Sorenson, S. (2013, June). *How employee engagement drives growth: Engaged companies outperform their competition, a Gallup study shows.* Retrieved from http://www.gallup.com/businessjournal/163130/employee-engagement-drives-growth.aspx

Deloitte University Press (2015). Global Human Capital Trends 2015. *Leading in the new world of work.*

Hewitt, A. (2013). *2013 Trends in global employee engagement.* London, UK: Aon plc.

Watson, T. (2013). *Clear direction in a complex world: How top companies create clarity, confidence, and community to build sustainable performance.* New York, NY.

Berthiaume, D. (2013, February 4). Temkin Group: Employee engagement rises, and that's a good thing. *CMSWire.* Retrieved from http://www.cmswire.com

Kruse, K. (2012). *Employee engagement 2.0: How to motivate your team for high performance (a "real world" business guide for busy managers).* Richboro, PA: The Kruse Group./Users/stephaniehuffman/Library/Containers/com.apple. Preview/Data/Desktop/CINDY/BW.chartsandgraphs/Chapter4.Operating-Margin.jpg

Royal, M., & Yoon, J. (2009). Engagement and enablement: The key to higher levels of individual and organizational performance. *Journal of Compensation and Benefits,* 13-19.

Perrins, T. (2003). *Working today: Understanding what drives employee engagement.* New York, NY.

Hewitt, A. (2014). *2014 Trends in global employee engagement.* London, UK: Aon plc.

Gallup, Inc. (2013). *State of the global workplace: Employee engagement insights for business leaders worldwide.* Retrieved from http://ihrim.org/Pubonline/Wire/Dec13/GlobalWorkplaceReport_2013.pdf

Schatsky, D., & Schwartz, J. (2015). *Global human capital trends 2015: Leading in the new world of work.* Deloitte University Press.

Kotter, J. P., & Heskett, J. L. (2011). *Corporate culture and performance.* New York, NY: The Free Press.

Chapter 5

Lipp, D. (2013). *Disney U: How Disney University develops the world's most engaged, loyal, and customer-centric employees.* New York: NY: McGraw-Hill.

Chapter 6

Mankins, M. C. (2013, December). Organizational culture: The defining elements of a winning culture. *Harvard Business Review.* Retrieved from https://hbr.org

Sinek, S. (2009). *Start with why: How great leaders inspire everyone to take action.* New York, NY: Penguin Group.

Luttrell, M. (2007). *Lone survivor: The eyewitness account of Operation Redwing and the lost heroes of SEAL Team 10.* New York, NY: Little, Brown and Company.

Hsieh, T. (2010). *Delivering happiness: A path to profits, passion, and purpose.* Mundelein, IL: Grand Central Publishing.

Golway, Terry (2005). *Washington's General: Nathaniel Greene and the Triumph of the American Revolution.* New York, Holt.

Frisch, Bob (2008). "When Teams Can't Decide" *Harvard Business Review,* November 1, 2008.

Gostick, A. and Elton, C. (2010). *The Orange Revolution: How One Great Team Can Transform an Entire Organization.* New York, NY: OC Tanner Company.

Chapter 7

Cohen, R. (2014). How the NFL reflects American culture. *The Wall Street Journal.* Retrieved from http://www.wsj.com

Chapter 8

Maxwell, J. C., & Dornan, J. (1997). *Becoming a person of influence.* Nashville, TN: Thomas Nelson.

Cloud, H., & Townsend, J. (1992). *Boundaries: When to say yes, how to say no, to take control of your life.* Grand Rapids, MI: Zondervan.

Chapter 9

Bradt, G., & Vonnegut, M. (2009). *Onboarding: How to get your new employees up to speed in half the time.* Hoboken, NJ: John Wiley & Sons.

Cross, Robert L. & Parker, A. (2004) *The Hidden Power of Social Networks,* Harvard Business School Publishing

Chapter 10

Maxwell, J. C. (1998). *The 21 irrefutable laws of leadership: Follow them and people will follow you.* Nashville, TN: Thomas Nelson.

Whole Foods Market (Producer & Host). (2014, October 19). Values Matter

[Video file]. *Values   Matter Anthem*. Retrieved from https://www.youtube. com/watch?v=5DCow4J-pDE

Dominos (Producer & Host). (2015, February). *Domino's TV Spot, 'Name Change.'* Retrieved from http://www.ispot.tv/ad/7xnm/ dominos-name-change

Ashkanasy, N. M., Wilderom, C. P. M., & Peterson, M. F. (2000). *Handbook of organizational culture and climate*. Thousand Oaks, CA: Sage Publications.

Chapter 11

Deal, J. J. (2013). *Always on, never done? Don't blame the smartphone*. Greensboro, NC: The Center for Creative Leadership.

Good Technology. (2012). *Good technology survey reveals Americans are working more, but on their own schedule*. Sunnyvale, CA.

American Psychological Association. (2013). *Americans stay connected to work on weekends, vacation and even when out sick*. Washington, DC.

Smith, A. (2012). *The best (and worst) of mobile connectivity*. Washington, DC: Pew Research Center. Creating a risk-taking culture in a risk-adverse environment [Web log post]. (2010, April 14). Retrieved from https://greatworkplace.wordpress.com/2010/04/14/ creating-a-risk-taking-culture-in-a-risk-averse-environment/

Day, G. S. (2013). *Innovation prowess: Leadership strategies for accelerating growth*. Philadelphia, PA: Wharton Digital Press.

Afterword

Maxwell, J.C. (2002) *The Maxwell Leadership Bible,* Thomas Nelson.

CPSIA information can be obtained at www.ICGtesting.com
Printed in the USA
BVOW06s0950300716

457022BV00007B/193/P